THE BAIKIE CHARIVARI

Theatre editions of James Bridie's plays

The Anatomist
Babes in the Wood
The Black Eye
Colonel Wotherspoon
Daphne Laureola
Dr. Angelus
It Depends What You Mean
Jonah and the Whale
King of Nowhere
The Last Trump
Mary Read
(with Claude Gurney)
Marriage is no Joke
Mr. Bolfry
Mr. Gillie
The Queen's Comedy
A Sleeping Clergyman
Storm in a Teacup
Susannah and the Elders
What Say They?
The Switchback
Tobias and the Angel

The above list is complete, but the publishers
cannot undertake that every book will
be available at any given time.

JAMES BRIDIE

(*Photo: Lida Moser, New York.*)

JAMES BRIDIE

THE BAIKIE CHARIVARI

or

THE SEVEN PROPHETS

A Miracle Play

With a portrait frontispiece
and a Preface by the Rt. Hon. Walter Elliot
C.H. M.P. F.R.S. etc.

CONSTABLE · LONDON

LONDON

PUBLISHED BY
Constable and Company Ltd.
IO–I2 ORANGE STREET, W.C.2

•

INDIA
Orient Longmans Ltd.
BOMBAY   CALCUTTA   MADRAS

•

CANADA
Longmans, Green and Company
TORONTO

•

SOUTH and EAST AFRICA
Longmans, Green and Company Ltd.
CAPE TOWN   NAIROBI

First published 1953

Printed in Great Britain by
RICHARD CLAY AND COMPANY, LTD.
BUNGAY
SUFFOLK

BRIDIE'S LAST PLAY

By WALTER ELLIOT

The Baikie Charivari was Bridie's last play. For this reason alone, it would be of moment to Scottish letters—which have a record of some importance to the artistry and thought of the rest of the world. It is also in itself one of the most noteworthy of the Bridie plays. It is really a companion to another piece, *The Queen's Comedy*, published two years earlier, in 1950. Bridie, in his own view, had come by this time to the limit of his accomplishments. He left amongst his papers certain short poignant verses beginning "It's time I was awa'"; and in the summer before he died, he had said in plain terms "There will be no more plays."

Whether that suggestion, on the lips of one to whom writing came as naturally as breathing, would ever have been true, we may venture to doubt. But it is accurate to say that, as far as the stage was concerned, he felt that he had reached the end of the road.

The Queen's Comedy is about the Gods. *The Baikie Charivari* is about men; or rather, about man, and therefore also about the Devil, the Opponent of man, who is called in our country sometimes the Enemy of Mankind, sometimes the Adversary, sometimes simply the De'il, according to the aspect which he presents. Bridie was well qualified, both by birth and by training, to consider this question. There is no place where you will encounter the hostility of fate at closer quarters than in the practice of medicine, at which he spent most of his life. It runs through his mind from his earliest plays—such as *The Sunlight Sonata*—until his end.

Furthermore, this theme has always pre-occupied Scottish thought, to the verge of obsession. There is a proverb in Europe, variously phrased, that you talk in English to horses, in Italian to women, and in Spanish to God. One might add a codicil that if you talk to the Devil, or about the Devil, you talk, unless you are Milton, in Scots. (There are those who claim that this can be equally well done in German. But this is not so; and if you doubt it, compare that seedy conjuror, Mephistopheles, with the Muckle Black De'il.) In fact, the Devil inspires a greater proportion of thought and writing amongst the Scots than amongst any other people; except, perhaps, the Hebrews. But amongst the Hebrews the Devil goes by the name of Satan, and figures in the company of the Sons of God. In Scotland he stands beyond all hierarchies.

To come to his problem, Bridie had to clear his stage of the Gods. He did this in *The Queen's Comedy*. It has on its title-page Gloucester's couplet from " Lear "

" As flies to wanton boys are we to the Gods
    They kill us for their sport."

The revealing fact is, that in both of these plays, the end is a disproof of the whole philosophy which these lines set forth.

The Queen's Comedy follows one of Bridie's favourite devices, that of an old tale told anew. It is a dramatisation from the Fourteenth and Fifteenth Books of the *Iliad*. The Queen of the title is Hera, Queen of Heaven, inspirer and deserter of mortals; wife to Zeus, Father of Gods and Men—Juno and Jupiter in the play, names which Bridie used only for the sake of a swifter dramatic impact.

During most of the play the acts of Gods and men alike are such as to justify up to the hilt the cry of blinded Gloucester. Then, for a few minutes before the end, four mortals, netted, by the curiosity of the Gods, out of a convoy of the shades hurrying from the battlefield to their appointed place, confront and accuse Heaven. The Gods are conscience-stricken. But Jupiter, having watched the scene for a little time, enters the field. He speaks, not with

the accents of Olympus, but in a more ancient and altogether more compelling tongue, that of the Unknown God
of the biologists.   The speech hushes the characters, Gods
and men alike.   It hushes the audience.   It gives, shortly
and ruthlessly, the picture of a creator, an author, driven
by an urge not under his control, to engender a creation
beyond his comprehension, but instinct with characters as
important to him as he to them.   This Unknown God
speaks neither in wrath nor, certainly, in pity; but in
some strange form of kinship, though remote and salt as
the sea.

Such a presentation repels many.   It attracts others.
But it is assuredly poles asunder from any kind of brow-
beating or persecution, or wanton sport.   Detachment,
true; but the detachment of an artist from his figures, of a
parent from his offspring.

The unresolved riddle of *The Queen's Comedy*, however,
lies in the acquiescence of everyone concerned.   It is made
explicit in a scrap of verse, the song of the scene-shifters,
as the play is about to begin.

" We are the scene-shifters. . . .
     We heaved up the Pyramids;
     We dinged doon Persepolis;
     We hung the Hanging Gardens;
     We made Atahualpa's Palace,
     And here one for Solomon,
     And there one for Semiramis.
         Hamburg and Hiroshima
     We blasted into shards.
     All contracts promptly and efficiently
     Executed.
     At the behest of the Immortal Gods
     Or of anyone else who likes giving orders . . ."

Where are the rebels ?   We have seen Zeus.   Where is
Prometheus ?

The Baikie Charivari is about mortals, and here the rebels
come to the centre of the picture.   The hero is Punch,

their legendary protagonist. But the play being about mortals, and mortals in Scotland at that, Bridie has to place in the forefront of the action the Devil, the endless enmity to humanity and all its works, which is one of the evident factors in the make-up of our affairs, including the make-up of man himself. Wells perceived this malevolence at the end of his days, and seeing, turned his face to the wall and died. He had conceded to it, to the Devil, the first place. We Scots deny him this topmost rank. But the Enemy, the Accuser of the Brethren, towers above everything but that. Whether he towers above man, especially man the rebel, is the question which never ceases to haunt us.

Again Bridie uses his device of the old tale told anew. But, as the protagonist has to be a good man as well as a rebel, to be a hero, Punch is incarnated as Sir James MacArthur Pounce-Pellott, K.C.I.E., sometime District Commissioner of Junglipore and other places, an administrator, a maker of order, in his time and place a King and a Priest; who has retired to Baikie, a little seaside resort on the Clyde estuary, to adapt himself, his wife, and daughter, to the 20th century in the West. There, naturally, he meets the other characters of the legend, the Beadle, the Hangman, the Dog, the Clown, the Doctor, the Ghost, Jim Crow and the Policeman; all, also, in modern guise—and, being in a Bridie play, considerably cut about. That the Hangman, Jack Ketch, should be a red-head, an electrician, a town councillor and a Communist, is no great leap; but Jim Crow, now Jemima, from Stubbs, Spottsville, Virginia, at first a witch and then a publisher's agent, is rather more outrageous.

Punch, by the way, in stage tradition, is also Pontius Pilate, so this strand also has been woven into his being; and if you boggle at this for a good man, remember that not only was Pilate, in Bridie's view, an upright administrator and an upholder of the *Pax Romana*, but that he is canonised in the Church of Abyssinia amongst the earliest

saints. In any case, the play is about the pursuit, by Evil,
of a good man; there is no drama in seeing the Devil
collect his own.

Authority is given for his harrying, and, if possible, his
destruction, in the Prologue. Enter, as the curtain rises,
the Devil, in full power. After the Prologue, comes reality;
and the play then moves forward simultaneously on the
two planes of fantasy and reality. The reality is that of
the little Clydeside town, with its minister, its tradesmen,
its doctor—a lady psychologist—and all the rest, including
the visitor from Stubbs, Spottsville, Virginia, Jemima
Crowe. It is shot through with the fantasy of the Punch
characters; at times there is interference between the
one plane and the other; elsewhere, they are wholly
independent.

The two planes blend at the play's finish. The Devil
comes, as in the puppet-show, to carry Punch away. But
by now, as before on Olympus, the puppet-show has
transformed itself. Punch has slain all his enemies. He
admits his crimes but justifies his deeds. Bridie and his
last character stand face to face.

" Have you come to take me ? " says Punch.

" I was wondering," says the De'il. " I'm thinking
you've jouked me for the moment. It may be you've
jinked me a' thegither ! "

And he vanishes.

There was a different Devil, still further North, the
Button-Moulder of Ibsen, who, coming to melt down
another Pontius, Peer Gynt, also adjourned, to an in-
definite date, the final encounter. Ibsen left the last word
to the Button-Moulder and to the blind Solveig. Odd
though it may seem, from Ibsen, Peer Gynt was going to
be saved by the love of a good woman. Bridie will allow
no such refuge to his hero.

" Time will tell us," says the De'il.

" Can I wait for time ? " says the hero.

" I dinna ken," says the De'il.

"If you don't know, who knows?" exclaims Pounce-Pellott.

"Nobody knows. Nobody knows.
I've killed all those fools who pretended to know.
And so . . . and so . . .
With the soothsayers littered about the stage
That I slew in my rage,
Who did not know . . . and no more do I . . .
I must jest again, and await my reply . . .
Good-bye."

I must jest again, says Mr. Punch. He has defeated his foes with his stick, and exorcised the Devil with his incantation. He finds himself, for all that, no nearer truth. But he has still the heart to jest again, and the conviction that the question has a reply.

This denouement leaves a vast, empty stage; and, though why I do not know, a great satisfaction. After *The Queen's Comedy* and *The Baikie Charivari*, what folly to say that Bridie could not write a last act . . .

You may say this is too fine-drawn, too metaphysical, and obviously too complicated, ever to make a play. Of that, future audiences must judge for themselves. Forget all you have read here. It is no more necessary to know the anatomy of a play than to know the skeleton of a man, in order to enjoy either. Begin at the Prologue, between the De'il and the Beadle. If you can read broad Scots, and wish to confirm what has been said about its being the natural speech of the De'il, read also *The Sunlight Sonata*, the first of all the Bridie plays, and the soliloquy with which it opens; the De'il in a storm on Loch Lomondside intoning hexameters into the night.

"Give me the bonny wee glens with the quick brown
     whispering water,
And Life in the burn, in the linn, by the river shadowed
     with cities.
Life in the muir and the wood and the clachan—
     flittering, fighting.

The rat and the bat and the dog; the otter, the owl
    and the adder;
The lean sculduddery cat and the slaters under the
    ruckies;
Maggots in dead men' eye-sockets; eels in the deep
    cold loch;
The sweating caird and his wife and weans in bed in
    the bothy
Wi' the plaid well over the lugs for fear of my wise
    horngollochs.
That peek and peer and hirple and crawl in their
    armour
Into the ears and the nose and the eyes and into the
    brain-pan
Into the very soul."

or the short gleeful lines

" You're feart o' me, you're feart o' me,
    Droll wee slug wi' the shifty e'e !
    Raise your praise to the Ancient of Days
    I prevent you in all your ways " . . .

If you do not concede, as some of us do, most whole-
heartedly, the word genius, to Bridie, you will agree at
least that he possessed a most unexpected and a most
original mind.

So take this play as it comes. Take the scenes of modern
comedy, Jack Ketch, the red-head electrician and Toby
Messan, his eighteen-year-old assistant, versus Lady
Pounce-Pellott, after her passage from India, who resents
their disrespectful bearing over the repair of her electric fire.
In fantasy, take the witches' coven, with Lady Maggie
Revenant, the Ghost; the lady-doctor psychologist, Miss
Pothecary; Joey Mascara, the Clown as its Officer, and
Jemima Crowe, coming " to bring sororial greetings from
the Alpha Beta Phi Coven of Stubbs, Spottsville, Virginia, a
coven of quite respectable antiquity, going back as it does,
to the days of the Puritan Fathers "—and their attempt
to betray a Maiden (who is Baby, the daughter) to the

infernal powers. Or take the transposition into the
realist key of Jemima Crowe, in the later acts, where, as
a publisher's agent, but still an emissary of the Devil,
she offers Sir James $7,000, $10,000, $200,000, for his
Indian reflections on the Decline and Fall of the British
Empire, so they be juicy enough.

> " Trumpets and elephants and cloth of gold . . .
> Trumpets and cloth of gold . . .
> Gold . . . gold . . . gold "

says Pounce-Pellott in his temptation. Which, in the event,
he finally overcomes.

It will take you quite a while. Each mouthful has to be
chewed forty times. . . . But worth it.

This play has actually been presented once, greatly
daring, by the Citizens' Theatre Company of Glasgow.
It will, without doubt, be presented again and again, for
it is a standing challenge to the stage; a challenge in
which anyone is more likely to fail than to succeed.

Here is Peer Gynt, of Scotland.

NOTE ON THE BAIKIE CHARIVARI

THERE is a tradition that the celebrated character of PUNCH is a projection of Pontius Pilate. The connection between the two characters is loose and fantastic, and probably depends on the fact that they are both regarded as important and symbolic murderers.

I have attempted to draw them together and, in that act, have probably diminished PUNCH's homicidal stature; but that cannot be helped. The synthesis takes place on the stage, of which PUNCH is an undoubted master. There are only two ways with traditional characters. One must denigrate them or whitewash them. I have, perhaps, whitewashed PUNCH in my natural desire to put a little punch into Pontius; but that cannot be helped. PUNCH can still hold his own, no matter who plays him down.

I understand that Pontius Pilate ran into no end of trouble, on more occasions than the remarkable One Occasion, in his efforts to keep the Roman Eagle upstanding. But we cannot help feeling that he was essentially a " good " man, and indifferent honest, according to his lights. Further, in all the circumstances, he was probably right; and it was his misfortune that he was cast for the villain of the piece in a play where virtue was, mainly by his act, triumphant. That is, if we are to believe the Apostle Paul.

Anyhow, he had a strong perception that he was bearing the White Man's Burden, and it is not for us to say that his perception was wrong.

Anyhow again, he makes not a bad prototype for the well-meaning, intelligent, devoted instruments of the Pax Britannica, which is equally hated by its enemies and its beneficiaries and seems now to have faded out. It is to be said, however, that amid all the welter of sociological theories, many of us are still utterly persuaded that Britain rose from the azure wave at Heaven's command and that it still has a sense of its vocation and responsibilities—that it invented Democracy (in its non-pejorative sense); and that it is still prepared to interpret Democracy according to the revelation granted only to Britain.

Another tradition is that Pontius was a Scotsman. Therefore he adds to his emotional awareness of his mission a proportion of ratiocinative awareness. I do not know how much there is in that. It seems to me to help the story in its aspect as a bit of entertainment.

The sun may have set on the British Empire, but do let us make use of the afterglow to read the Book of Fate.

J. B.

The play was first presented by the Glasgow Citizens' Theatre at the Royal Princess's Theatre on 6th October 1952 with the following cast:

THE DE'IL	James Gibson
THE REV. DR. MARCUS BEADLE	Roddy Macmillan
ROBERT COPPER . .	Alasdair Urquhart
SIR JAMES MACARTHUR POUNCE-PELLOTT,	
K.C.I.E.	Donald Eccles
COUNCILLOR JOHN KETCH .	Andrew Keir
TOBY MESSAN . . . ·	Michael Elder
MISS POUNCE-PELLOTT . .	. Iris Russell
LADY POUNCE-PELLOTT . .	Ursula Jeans
JOE MASCARA . . .	George Cole
DR. JEAN POTHECARY .	Madeleine Christie
LADY MAGGIE REVENANT .	Marillyn Gray
MRS. JEMIMA LEE CROWE .	Marion Mathie

The play was produced by Peter Potter
Settings designed by John Wilson

PERSONS

SIR JAMES MacARTHUR POUNCE-PELLOTT, K.C.I.E.

LADY POUNCE-PELLOTT (JUDY)

MISS POUNCE-PELLOTT (BABY)

THE REV. DR. MARCUS BEADLE

COUNCILLOR JOHN KETCH

JOE MASCARA

TOBY MESSAN

DR. JEAN POTHECARY

MRS. JEMIMA LEE CROWE

ROBERT COPPER

LADY MAGGIE REVENANT

THE DE'IL

———

TIME : The Present

PLACE : Baikie, on the Clyde Estuary

The Play is divided into a Prologue and Two Acts

The Characters are entirely imaginary

———

THE BAIKIE CHARIVARI

PROLOGUE

A Drop Scene represents a hillside crowded with bungalows. They rise to a dark, stormy sky with a huge moon. The middle bungalow, at stage level, has a big, dark window, which can light up later, and a faint light glimmering through the fanlight. This is BAIKIE, *in its less fashionable quarter. It is, of course, night and the season is November. The audience is sitting on the edge of a restless sea, which may or may not be indicated by a susurrus from a loud-speaker at the back of the pit. A short Punch and Judy, Anniversaire-du-bébé Overture continues after the rise of the Curtain, and is blended with the growing and fading sounds of a nocturnal cat fight. Sea sounds go on monotonously, fading when the Characters begin to speak.*

[*Suddenly a big* DEVIL MASK *appears in the moon.*

THE DE'IL. Thrum away, thrum along, Polyphlosboios.
Lustrate the shores of Baikie my Beloved.
This is my Baikie.
A slate-grey township half as old as Peckham,
Grew in Italian villas, built in the fifties,
And Scots baronial mansions
Handy by train for the City,
For shipbuilders, stockbrokers, wholesale grocers to
   die in,
Lulled by the wash of the waves of the Clyde
And soothed by the sicht of white sails and the cries
   of the sea birds—
Baikie, my own, my Beloved.
No sae genteel, these days, no sae genteel;

B   [1]

When the bungaloids burgeon and gowfers gowf
And keelies squeal on the foreshore
And screwtaps gang crash on the rocks and the
reeking omnibuses belch;
But aye the Jewel o' the Tail o' the Bank where the
tall ships anchor.
In the morning train the Scots Baron aye nods to the
Bungalist
(Providing their wives are na with them),
And the baith o' them lippen to me, the son of the
morning and evening,
O Baikie, my Beloved, my washpot, my own.

[THE DE'IL *vanishes as—*

[*A* BEADLE *and a* POLICEMAN *enter from opposite sides.*

[*The* BEADLE *is* DR. BEADLE, *and the* POLICEMAN *is* MR. COPPER; *but we only learn this later. In the dim light they appear to be dressed like Punch and Judy characters.*

BEADLE. Good evening, Constable.

POLICEMAN. Is that yourself, Doctor Beadle? You're early afoot.

BEADLE. Aye. I couldna get sleep.

POLICEMAN. A pity, that.

BEADLE. Will it be a good day, do you think?

POLICEMAN. I wouldna wonder. It's mild for November.

BEADLE. Good morning, then.

POLICEMAN. Good morning.

[*Exit* POLICEMAN.

[*The moon turns red and* THE DE'IL'*s voice comes from it.*

THE DE'IL. Hae ye considered my servant Pounce-Pellott?
There isna his marrow in a' the yerd—

[2]

A wyse, independent, sel'-saining carle,
Wha gangs his gate and lippens to nane,
And spiers at his hert when the lift is smoored.
Hae ye gi'en thocht tae my servant, Pounce?

BEADLE. Aye, he's honest eneugh, and what for no?
Cantie and douce in cosy bit house
Wi' a decent like spouse and a bairn to cheer him
And naething ava in the warld to steer him.
Whatfor should he ettle for a sidelins gate,
Wi' a dram in his aumry, a bite on his plate.
The lave would be cantie in siccan a state.

THE DE'IL. Siccar eneugh. Siccar eneugh.
Is't your will we should coup him intil the sheugh?
Be it so then, my bonny bit Beadle.
Tak' your will o' the birkie and a' that is his.
Daunton him, dozen him. Ca' him doon.
Smite him wi' tetters frae the tap to the croon.
And we'll see. Syne we'll see.

BEADLE. Almichty and Everlasting, Eternal, Unseen,
I jalouse what you're after. I ken what ye mean.
I'll see gin I can shake his Spiritual Pride—
The Sin that ca'ed Lucifer doon in his stride—
The unpardonable and imponderable Sin o' all Sins.
I'll click his kyboes. I'll kick his shins.
Wi' Thy sovran aid, I'll tame the billie,
Or will he, or nil he.
I'll awa tae my vestry and think and think.
A nod, ony day, is as guid as a wink
To Marcus John Beadle, Doctor o' Divinity,
Particular gin it come fra Unfathomable Infinity.
Like Saint Paul in his fit on the road to Damascus,
I hae my plain orders. I ken what my task is.
I ken, Lord, I ken.
To Thee be the Glory. Amen and Amen.

[*Exit* BEADLE.

[THE DE'IL *reappears*.

[3]

THE DE'IL. Aye, to me be the glory, ye Reverend
Tumphie.

I hid my face from ye and maybe it was as weel.

It's ill to thole for a man of God, the physog o' the
De'il.

It's no a bonny like pan for a man of God to view.

It's no a bonny like errand I've set you in train to do.

But you're only the yin wi' his slabbering neb to the
track.

I maun get me a hantle mair hellhounds to fill up my
pack,

And he'll gie us a run for our money.   He'll gie us a
run;

But we'll chase him and catch him and pu' him doon,
ere the long day is done.

Hoho, hoho.   The cock doth crow.

Fiat, fiat. I go. I go.

> [*The cock crows and* THE DE'IL *vanishes.*

> [*Dawn Music as the stage lightens a little, but not much.
> The big window in the middle bungalow lights up, and a
> really good tenor voice is heard singing* Lucevan le
> stelle *from* Tosca—*one or two of the more heart-
> rending bars—then the blind snaps up and shows* SIR
> JAMES POUNCE-PELLOTT *in a dressing-gown, shaving
> himself and whistling the remainder of the passage.
> He is a good-looking man in his early fifties.*

P.-P. They still shine across the wine dark waters, the
late lamps of Port Girning and Plannock.   They'll soon
be drowned in the grey of another dubious dawn. (*He
whistles another bit of* Tosca.)

Here I am, James MacArthur Pounce-Pellott, Knight
Commander of the Indian Empire, King of Ghosts and
Shadows, sometime District Commissioner of Junglipore
and other places.

I am the son of Major Hamish Pounce-Pellott, late of

the Dandy Ninth and of his wife, Grizel MacArthur. They have both been a long time dead.

I was born at Fortingall in Perthshire like my ancestor, Pontius Pilate, Procurator of Judea, Samaria and Idumea.

My predestinate fate has been not unlike his. But they did not allow me to wait for a reply. I did not wash my hands of the Mahatma. He washed his hands of me.

So here I am at Baikie in my new little chrysalis bungalow lapped in my little pension, with all my old life behind me, waiting to learn the new life.

Who will teach me the ways of the new life ? I am eager to learn.

JUDY (*off*). Your bath's running, Jimmie.

P.-P. All right, dear; I'm just coming.

> [*He towels his face and switches off the light. Presently a smaller window lights up and splashing and* The Flower Song *from* Carmen *are heard, as the grey dawn breaks.*

END OF PROLOGUE

ACT I

*Lounge–parlour–breakfast–dining-room at Taj Mahal, Baikie,
the residence of* SIR JAMES MACARTHUR POUNCE-PELLOTT.
*It is part of a five room and kitchen bungalow, 1930 vintage.
The furniture, fittings and distempered walls are like those
of other bungalows of the same sort—strictly neutral and in
ghastly good taste; but some of the gorgeous East has spilled
into the room, and there are plenty of ivory ornaments, brass
trays, inlaid tables, elephants' tusks and a huge tiger-skin
rug. There are enlarged signed photographs of King
George V and Queen Mary.*

> [*In front of the built-in electric fire,* COUNCILLOR JOHN
> KETCH *and* TOBY MESSAN *are kneeling. They have
> torn a good chunk out of the wall to expose the wiring,
> and there is a heap of detritus on a dust-sheet.* TOBY
> *is packing the tools.* KETCH *is an angry-looking
> red-head of thirty odd.* TOBY *is an earnest-looking,
> depressed sort of lad of eighteen.*

KETCH. There now. That's about the best we can
do. (*He switches on the fire.*) It's all we're bloody well
going to do, anyway.

TOBY. Aye.

KETCH. What's the time?

TOBY. Quarter-past four.

KETCH. There's a fine demonstration of the kinno' a
job your fine private enterprise puts up. It's a wonder
the whole biling of them wasna electrocuted. Maybe they
will be yet, and no great loss.

> [*Enter* MISS POUNCE-PELLOTT (BABY), *a pretty girl of
> about seventeen, in pyjamas and a dressing-gown.*

BABY. Oh, sorry.

[6]

[She finds a box of sugared fruits and goes out with it.

KETCH.   There goes a bitch.

TOBY.   I don't know.

KETCH.   You know fine.   Dancing all night and no' up
and dressed at four in the afternoon.   Pack of parasites.
(*He lights a cigarette.*)   Never mind.   It'll no' be long now.

TOBY.   No.

KETCH.   She'll no' get her lipstick and her bath salts
and her sweltering between sheets all day in the labour
camp.

TOBY.   No.

KETCH.   And the Sirs and the Ladyships'll attend to
their ain wiring, if they can.   Trash !

[Voices in the passage.

JUDY (*off*).   I'm so sorry.   I don't think the tradesmen
have gone yet. . . .   Do you mind waiting a minute ?

KETCH.   Tradesmen !

BEADLE (*off*).   Not at all.   Not at all.   Not at all.

[Enter LADY POUNCE-PELLOTT (JUDY).   *Handsome.*
Forty.

JUDY.   Have you finished ?

KETCH.   I've done the best I can.   You'll need to have
the whole installation pulled out by the roots before it's
safe.   But I suppose it will have to do.

JUDY.   Are you going to leave all that mess ?

KETCH.   That's a plasterer's job.   I'm a plumber and
electrician.

JUDY.   It's disgraceful.

KETCH.   It is, is it ?

JUDY.   And what in the world do you mean by coming
at this time of day ?

KETCH.   If you've got nothing to do all day, I've got
plenty.

JUDY.   Need you be impertinent ?

KETCH.   You don't like my manners, eh?

JUDY.   Not very much, I'm afraid.

KETCH.   You'd better go back to your kitmatghars and your dhoolie wallahs, then.   You'll no' get workers here to bump their brow on the grun three times to the likes of you. (*He flicks his ash on the carpet.*)   You'll get nae sycophancy from me.

JUDY.   I suppose we've got to thank the Labour Government for this sort of thing?

KETCH.   You needna bother thanking them.   I'm a Communist.

JUDY (*mastering herself*).   Have you finished what you were doing?

KETCH.   I told you I had.

JUDY.   Then, will you kindly go?

KETCH.   Aye, I'm going all right.   Come on, Toby. You're getting between the wind and her Ladyship's nobility.

> [*Exeunt* KETCH *and* TOBY.   TOBY *touches his cap in a furtive kind of way.*

> [*Voices in passage.*

(*Off*).   Hello, Mr. Beadle.

BEADLE.   Hello, Councillor.   How are you?

KETCH.   Fine.   How's the beauty of holiness?

BEADLE.   Awa wi' ye, ye Bolshevik rascal!

> [*Door slams.*

JUDY.   Come in, Doctor Beadle.

> [*As* BEADLE, *a rather ascetic-looking Parson, enters,* JUDY *gathers up the dust-sheet by its four corners.*

JUDY.   I suppose I needn't apologise.   You must be used to this sort of thing.   I'm afraid I'm not properly oriented yet.

BEADLE.   That's all right, Lady Pounce-Pellott.   That's quite all right.

JUDY.   Take a seat.   Do excuse me.

[*Exit* JUDY *with dust-sheet.*

[BEADLE *strolls around looking at the curios, and humming a Psalm tune.   Re-enter* JUDY.

There now.

[THEY *sit.*

Oh, dear.

BEADLE.   He's rather a rough diamond, is Ketch. Quite a decent fellow, though, in his own way.   He's a Town Councillor.   Quite an important fellow.   He's rather a menace, of course, but I quite like him.

JUDY.   I'm afraid I'm not educated up to him.   Will you have some tea ?

BEADLE.   No, no, no, no, no.   You mustn't dream of troubling.

JUDY.   Shall we have it when Polly comes in ?   He's my husband.   He's gone for a walk along the beach. He'll be in any time now.

BEADLE.   How does Sir James like Baikie ?

JUDY.   Well, we haven't quite settled down yet.   We've only just got our bits of things in.   He likes the sea.

BEADLE.   Ah.   The sea.   Yes.   Baikie's a quiet little place.   It must be a great change for you all.

JUDY.   Yes, it is.

BEADLE.   I hope when you've settled down we shall see you at the Kirk, now and again.

JUDY.   Yes.   We always went to the Scotch Church at Junglipore.   Jim thought it a good example.

BEADLE.   An excellent example.

JUDY.   Yes.

BEADLE.   Yes.

JUDY.   I think it helped Polly—Jim—with what he called his equilibrium, too.

BEADLE.   His equilibrium ?

JUDY.   Yes.   You see, in India he was a sort of King—

[9]

Sahib this and Huzoor that. Everybody sort of bathed
in his mild and magnificent eye. He thought it wasn't
good for him, you see. So he was terribly respectful to
God and the Viceroy and all that sort of thing. Though,
mind you, he hated it. He's a very proud man.

BEADLE. There is such a thing as proper pride. He was
doing splendid work.

JUDY. That was another thing. He had to equilibrate
that. Keep his feet on the ground, in a way. He *knew*
he was building up something terrific. But he knew too
that it might all tumble about his ears any day. So he put
in a bit of destruction too. To balance it. So he shot
tigers and stuck wild pig, although he hated it. He's an
extraordinary man in many ways. There was the risk,
too. He says he likes taking his own risks. It com-
pensates for the risks he can't help. He hates being
pushed about, even by Providence.

BEADLE. He can hardly help *that*.

JUDY. No. But he hates it. . . . Of course, when
really bad things happen, he takes them very well. He's
in training, you see. That time Baby fell overboard . . .

BEADLE. Baby?

JUDY. That's our daughter. We call her Baby. It's
rather silly.

BEADLE. She fell overboard? Into the sea?

JUDY. Oh, years ago. She really was a baby then.
We were coming home on leave. Jim was dancing her
up and down on the rail—to give her courage or something, and she jumped out of his arms. He dived in after
her; but he stunned himself when he hit the water. He
was nearly drowned. Luckily one of the greasers—a
Scotch boy—was looking out of a porthole—just above
the Plimsoll Line—and he jumped in and got Baby. So
neither of them was much the worse. I got the worst of
it. I've never been really fit since.

BEADLE. A terrible experience.

JUDY. Yes.

BEADLE. Your husband may dislike the ways of
Providence, but they are truly wonderful.

JUDY. Yes, aren't they? . . . We haven't seen the
greaser since. We gave him quite a lot of money and I
think he got a Humane Society Medal, but he simply
vanished when we got to Southampton. We couldn't
trace him.

BEADLE. What was his name?

JUDY. You'll think it terrible of me, but I've forgotten
it. Jim really tried to trace him; but we never talked
about it. Honestly, I couldn't bear to think . . . I can't
imagine why I'm telling you. There must be something
Father-Confessorish about you.

BEADLE. Well, we don't believe in the Confessional in
our Communion; but we realise, of course, that it is good
for the soul. I'm happy that you have told me.

JUDY. That abominable plumber must have upset me.
In a way it's much easier to be a King and Queen—though
there are responsibilities, too. At least one doesn't have
to fight for scraps of common civility.

[*Hall door opens.*

Oh, there's Polly . . . Polly!

P.-P. (*off*). Hello!

JUDY. We've got a visitor.

P.-P. Who is it?

JUDY. Come in.

P.-P. I've got one too. . . . Come along in, Mr.
Mascara . . .

[*Enter* SIR JAMES POUNCE-PELLOTT, *ushering in* JOE
MASCARA, *a youngish, Italianate man with a strong
Glasgow accent.*

P.-P. Mr. Mascara, my wife . . . (*To* BEADLE). How
do you do?

JUDY. This is Doctor Beadle.

BEADLE. How do you do?

P.-P.   This is quite a party, isn't it ? Where did you put the gin ?

JUDY.   I don't think the Doctor would like gin. Would you, Doctor ?

BEADLE.   I'm not a total abstainer; but not at this time of day, I think.

JUDY.   Tea, then ?

BEADLE.   I wouldn't dream of troubling you.

P.-P.   That's one of the two thousand formulæ for accepting a drink. Get him some tea, Judy. And where's the gin ? And where's that lazy little slut, Baby ?

JUDY.   In the cupboard. She's just getting up. I won't be a minute.

[*Exit* JUDY.

P.-P. (*preparing drinks*). Do make yourselves comfortable. Do you know each other ?

BEADLE (*aloof*). I have the pleasure of Mr. Mascara's acquaintance.

P.-P.   Good. *Will* you have a drink, Doctor Beadle ?

BEADLE.   No. I thank you.

JOEY.   Not in front of the kids. Mine's a straight gin.

P.-P.   I made Mr. Mascara's acquaintance on the promenade.

BEADLE.   I am not surprised.

P.-P. (*without appearing to notice his tone*). Lovely silver point effects on the loch today. I'll take up painting, I think.

BEADLE.   An innocuous occupation.

P.-P.   I suppose so, if it doesn't go to one's head.

BEADLE.   Quite.

P.-P. (*he has served the drinks and is settling down*). Well, well. So you are old friends ?

JOEY.   If you've a fancy to be accurate—no. I played the organ for a while in the Doctor's place of worship. We didna quite see eye to eye, did we, Doctor ?

BEADLE.   That's putting it mildly.

P.-P. I see.

JOEY. His Holiness doesna make allowances for the artistic temperament.

BEADLE. In some of its manifestations, I most certainly don't.

P.-P. What did you do, Joey?

BEADLE. What didn't he do?

JOEY. Ugh! It was nothing. He's quite right. It was no place for me.

P.-P. We ought to change the subject, you think?

BEADLE. It would certainly be better.

P.-P. I've no tact. Here's looking at you.

JOEY. Best respects, Sir James. . . . Though, mind you, what do the wee girls join the choir for, if it's not for a bit of fun?

BEADLE (*rising*). I'll call another time, Sir James, when you're not entertaining—company.

P.-P. No, no. I won't hear of it. I'll see that Mr. Mascara behaves himself.

JOEY. It's not as if they could sing.

P.-P. (*suddenly formidable*). Did you hear what I said?

JOEY. No offence.

P.-P. Do sit down, Doctor. . . . I'm most awfully glad you called. Did my wife tell you about me?

BEADLE. We had a little chat.

P.-P. We're like visitors from Mars. All this is entirely new to me. I'm beginning life all over again—from the start. It's most exhilarating.

BEADLE. In your new situation you must find many things a wee thing strange; but it's hardly beginning all over again.

P.-P. Yes, it is. I've decided to throw overboard everything I ever learned or knew. It's the only way. It's no good trying to fit round pegs into square holes. I've gone all malleable. I've gone all plastic. I'm wonderful material for a spiritual adviser. Would you like to be my spiritual adviser?

[13]

BEADLE.   We-e-e-ll, I have certain qualifications for that office.

P.-P.   Good.   I knew you had.   I made enquiries. You've got the job, if you want it.   Joey, here, is going to coach me in modern æsthetics.   There's no such thing as pure chance, is there ?   I expect a perfect shower of angels and guides.   The Lord threw down Joseph to me outside the municipal convenience, half an hour ago. I took it as a sign that my education was well in hand. Your arrival absolutely confirmed that.   I've just got to wait until they all arrive.   Splendid.   Joey, your glass is empty.

JOEY.   It is.   It is.

P.-P.   You won't change your mind, Doctor Beadle ?

BEADLE.   No.

P.-P.   I can't tell you how I'm looking forward to my education.

BEADLE.   They say education is the drawing out of in-born characteristics.   Ye seem to have a sense of humour.

P.-P.   It may seem so to you, but I haven't really.   I'm a very serious individual.   Only stupid people go giggling through life.   Life's a serious matter.   If I've got a sense of humour, you must help me to get rid of it.   I'm sure you will.

BEADLE.   Now, now.   You mustn't miscall your sense of humour.   It's like the pipes.   It puts lichtsomeness into your feet on many a stey brae.   I've a very strong sense of humour myself, and whiles I wonder what I would ever have done wanting it.

> [*This thought depresses* BEADLE *so much as to bring him near to tears.   He shakes his head sadly.*   MASCARA *nods in solemn agreement.*

JOEY (*suddenly*).   One of Scotia's chiefest glories
    Is her stock of funny stories.

BEADLE.   We can sense the bright hereafter
    In discreet and homely laughter.

[14]

JOEY.   The perception of the droll
   Is a poultice to the soul.
BEADLE.   Merriment (if it is pure)
   Is like sunshine on a sewer.
JOEY.   A sovran way of keeping fit
   Is to exercise one's wit.
BEADLE.   The grate of the eternal file
   Can be softened by a smile.
P.-P.   Dear me !

                         [*Enter* JUDY *with tea-tray.*

JUDY.   You all look very solemn.
P.-P.   We were discussing a very serious matter.
JUDY.   I'm sure you were. . . . My husband has no small talk.   He can only ask questions.   All sorts of questions. . . . Do you take sugar and milk, Doctor Beadle ?
BEADLE.   Both, please.
JUDY.   It was part of his job.   About the crops and the rains and where a Gurkha in the Guard of Honour got his medal.   Gracious questions.   Has he been asking you gracious questions, Mr. Mascara, and do you want any tea ?
JOEY.   No tea, thanks.   I don't think he's been catechising us much.   He . . .
JUDY.   He puts people so much at their ease that they go all paralysed.
JOEY.   He says he's got no sense of humour; but I'm sure he's pulling our legs.
JUDY.   Oh, he never, never does that.
P.-P.   I should think not.
JOEY.   That's all right, then.
P.-P.   Perfectly all right.   They are going to take my education in hand.   Isn't that kind of them ?
JUDY.   Very kind of them.   A tomato sandwich, Doctor ?
BEADLE.   I thank you. . . . I am afraid I approach the

education of a Balliol man, who is also a Knight Commander of the Indian Empire, with some trepidation.

P.-P. But there is no Indian Empire. It would not
surprise me in the least to learn that Balliol has dis-
appeared. I should be delighted to find that it had.
We want clear decks. A clean slate. A new start.

JUDY. I shall never get used to it, I'm afraid.

P.-P. But you must.

BEADLE. Lady Pounce-Pellott has just had a short
encounter with the new class-conscious democracy.

P.-P. Oh, good ! How did you get on ?

JUDY. The plumber was most impertinent.

BEADLE. You mustn't mind him. At heart, he's a very
decent fellow, Ketch.

JOEY. The Red Councillor ?

BEADLE. Yes.

JOEY. I bet you got your packet from Jack Ketch, Lady
Pellott.

P.-P. From whom ?

JOEY. Jack Ketch. Hanging Jack. He's quite a
character round here, old Ketchovich.

P.-P. But . . . but . . . it's not a very common name.

[*Enter* BABY.

JUDY. Oh, hello, Baby. You're up at last.

BABY. Yes.

JUDY. This is my daughter, Doctor Beadle. Mr.
Mascara.

BABY. How do you do ? Any tea ?

JUDY. You don't deserve any.

[BABY *collects tea and a few sandwiches, and sits apart
    from the* GROUP.

JOEY. Been ill ?

BABY. No.

JOEY. Had a thick night, then ?

BABY. A bittie.

[16]

JOEY.   Have you tried Faivre's cachets ?

BABY.   Yes.

BEADLE (*booming*).   Extraordinarily mild weather for November, Lady Pounce-Pellott.   But, coming from a warmer climate, you may not notice it.

JUDY.   It was sometimes very cold in Junglipore.

BEADLE.   So I have heard.   It's strange, but one looks on these oriental localities as being bathed in perpetual sunshine.

JOEY.   Hell's supposed to be hot, but they have to keep the fire burning continually.

BEADLE.   I'd prefer a little less profanity from you, Mr. Mascara.

JUDY.   But it *is* an interesting point of view, isn't it ?

BEADLE.   A point of view be interesting, and at the same time in very bad taste.

JUDY.   That's true, and it's a great pity.   Have another cup of tea ?

BEADLE.   Thank you.

[*A bell rings.*

JUDY.   Baby, see who that is, will you ?

[*Exit* BABY.

[POUNCE-PELLOTT *is in a brown study.*

I've often wondered about Hell.   I suppose it still exists, doesn't it ?

BEADLE (*with a glance at* JOEY).   It most assuredly does.

JUDY.   It's as well to know, isn't it ?

[*Re-enter* BABY, *introducing* DR. POTHECARY—*a hand-some, bouncing lady doctor of forty.*

BABY.   Doctor Pothecary, Mummy.

JUDY.   Oh, how do you do ?

POTHECARY.   Quite well.   I'm never ill, thank God. It wouldn't do these days, would it ?   Hello, Doctor Beadle.   Hello, Mr. Mascara.   It's not often we see the lion having a siesta with the lamb.

C   [17]

JOEY.   I'll be the lamb, I suppose.

POTHECARY.   " His fleece was black as soot," wasn't it ?
You'll be Sir James ?

JUDY.   Yes.   This is my husband.

POTHECARY.   Baikie's very highly honoured.   Pleased
to meet you.

P.-P.   How do you do ?

POTHECARY.   I thought I'd just drop in.

JUDY.   How nice of you.   Tea or gin ?

POTHECARY.   Tea . . . I'm terribly intrigued, Sir
James.   What made you retire to Baikie ?

P.-P.   I hardly know.   I thought I'd like to see the
river starting off for America and, anyhow, I'm half
Scotch.   I suppose one tends to return to one's mother
country.

POTHECARY.   Mother country, eh ?   That's interesting.
That's quite interesting, in a way.   Mother country . . .
(*Takes tea.*) . . . Thank you. . . . That's very interesting.

P.-P.   Is it ?   How ?

POTHECARY.   Oh, *you* know.   Regression to fœtal life,
and so on.

P.-P.   You're a psychologist, then ?

POTHECARY.   I've done a bit at it.   If a G.P. wants to
keep alive, she's got to have something else to turn to
besides signing forms for foundation garments.

P.-P.   You must tell me about psychology.   I've been
out of everything for a long time.

POTHECARY.   You must have been.   I'll tell you anything you like.   You might be better of a wee do over.
You were talking to yourself when I came in.

P.-P.   Was I ?

POTHECARY.   Yes.   We keep our eyes open, in my job.
What do you dream about ?

P.-P.   It's funny you should mention that.   Last night I
had a most extraordinary dream.   I thought I . . .

JUDY.   Polly, you mustn't.   This isn't a consulting
room.

POTHECARY. No. She's quite right. But we must have a session. I'd say offhand there was some mal-adjustment here. The wee lassie looks like death warmed up. . . . You don't look so bad, Lady Pellott. But maybe you're putting a good face on it.

JUDY. I do my best.

POTHECARY. It isn't always the best way. You should let yourself go, now and again. But, O please ! You mustn't think I'm touting for patients.

JUDY. Of course not. And I don't think we're a very promising field.

POTHECARY. You'd wonder. Even Doctor Beadle, there. He looks integrated enough; but if you were to turn him up like a flat stone, you'd find some peculiar things.

JUDY. O, Doctor, Doctor, you mustn't say things like that. Doctor Beadle's an authority on good taste. I don't think he'd give you very high marks. After all, it may be all right to make remarks about Doctor Beadle's Unconscious Mind; but you must have the time and the place and the loved one altogether. Mustn't you ?

POTHECARY. It's quite wrong to say that I'm in love with Doctor Beadle.

BEADLE. Dear me, I should think so.

POTHECARY. He's an obvious candidate for the Father Figure; but I've got rid of all that. You see, I've been psychoanalysed.

JUDY. That must have been very jolly for you.

POTHECARY. Jolly ? Not at all. Upon my word, Lady Pellott, if you're going to give me lectures on good taste . . . of course, there's no such thing, but all the same . . .

JUDY. I'm so sorry.

POTHECARY. Not at all. But even psychoanalysts have their feelings.

JUDY. I'll remember that in future.

POTHECARY.   It's a science.

JUDY.   I'm sure it is.

POTHECARY.   Very well, then. . . . Of course, it isn't in the least surprising that you should have a negative transference.

JUDY.   What is a negative transference?

POTHECARY.   Roughly, it means that you hate me.

JUDY.   But I don't.

POTHECARY.   Yes you do.   For goodness sake don't talk about things you know nothing about. . . . (*To the* OTHERS.)   I know you think it's a bit uncouth of me to be so blunt with a Ladyship; but social rank is nothing to me.   It's a bit of fetishism.   I'm a scientist, you see.   I can be completely objective about things like that.   Dukes and Duchesses and even Royalty are so many cases to me.   I must go now.   If you'd like to have a talk with me, Sir James, my number's in the book.   I am pretty certain I can help you.   Don't get up, anybody.   I'll find my way out.   Au revoir, everybody.

[P.-P. *opens the door for her and follows her out.*

JUDY.   Yes. . . . Is she a good Doctor?

BEADLE.   She has a very good name.   But some curious ideas.

JUDY.   I'm not sure that I like lady doctors.

JOEY.   I can see them being a bit embarrassing, sometimes.

BEADLE.   Intensely embarrassing.

BABY.   How?

JOEY.   Well, I mean to say!   Suppose she asks you to take your clothes off.

BABY.   I don't mind taking my . . .

JUDY.   Baby, be quiet! . . . At the same time, I can't help wondering whether " Lady Doctor " is quite an exact description. . . . Where has Polly got to?

JOEY.   He's seeing her out.

JUDY.   Oh!

JOEY.   You'd better mind your eye, Ma'am, lady or no lady.

JUDY.   What do you mean by that?

JOEY.   They tell me they've a very funny line of talk, those trick cyclists.   A bit exciting for middle-aged gents.

JUDY.   My husband and I are getting quite used to extraordinary " lines of talk," Mr. Mascara.

JOEY.   No offence.

JUDY.   I suppose not.   A cup of tea, Doctor Beadle?

BEADLE.   No, thank you.   Thank you very much. Indeed, it is time I was going.

JUDY.   Oh, but you mustn't go yet.   We're expecting another visitor.   Do you know her?   Lady Maggie Revenant?

BEADLE.   Oh, is she coming?

JUDY.   Yes.   Her brother was on the Viceroy's staff. I haven't met her; but she said she would call.

BEADLE.   A fine lady.   A fine lady, indeed.   If you don't mind, I'll wait a few minutes on the chance of having a word with her.

JUDY.   Of course.   You must wait.

BEADLE.   She lives here in quite a quiet way.   As you know, they had to sell Torrie Castle to the County Council —for mental defectives—death duties.   It's sad.   There will soon be no old families left.

JUDY.   No.   Nothing but mental defectives.

BEADLE.   A pity.

JUDY.   Yes.   It's a pity.

BEADLE.   They made for stability.

JUDY.   Yes.

BEADLE.   Lady Maggie is no inconsiderable poet—or, perhaps I should say, poetess.

JUDY.   Is she?   I'm afraid I don't know her.

BEADLE.   You'll like her.   I'm sure you'll like her. You will probably find a great deal in common.   Acquaintances and so on.

JUDY.   Yes.   We liked her brother.   It was sad about

him.   But I believe he's quite happy in the asylum.   Jim
went to see him when we got back. . . . Where *is*
Jim ?

[*Re-enter* POUNCE-PELLOTT.

P.-P.   Most interesting woman, that.

JUDY.   You seem to have found her so.

P.-P.   She says I'm an obsessional type.   Do you know,
I believe I am.

JUDY.   No, dear, you're not.

P.-P.   She was worried about Baby.

JUDY.   Was she ?

P.-P.   Yes.   Quite worried.   I told her about . . .
Well, I said I'd try to arrange for Baby to see her.   Do you
mind, honey ?

BABY.   It's all right by me.   I'll try anything once.

JOEY.   That's the spirit.

P.-P.   Doctor Beadle, the thing about this place is
that everybody is so extraordinarily kind.   I'm glad I
came.

BEADLE.   I'm glad of that.

P.-P.   I gave it a good deal of thought, and it looks as if I
were right in coming here.

BEADLE.   I hope you may find it so.

P.-P.   I didn't know a soul in Baikie; but I thought I'd
find a pretty good cross-section of the human race.

BEADLE.   You could describe it that way.

P.-P.   I think I *need* Baikie.

BEADLE.   And Baikie needs you, Sir James.

P.-P.   Oh, does it ?   Well . . . I'll have to get my
bearings first, as I told you.   I must get my bearings.

JOEY.   He has lost his bearings.   You heard what he
        said ?

    The points of the compass are dancing a reel round
        his head.

    He is lost.

    He is tumbled and tossed.

[22]

BEADLE.   We have an anchor that keeps the soul
  Steadfast and true while the billows roll.
JOEY.   Never heed him, Sir James, never heed him.
  You don't need him, Sir James, you don't need
    him.
  Throw yourself on the wind, it will carry you high.
  Jump against the wind and you'll fall or you'll fly.
  We should trust to our ears and our eyes and our
    hands like men.
  If we fall, what then ?
  It's better to die in a flash than be eaten by moths,
  Stifled by incense and smothered in altar cloths.
BEADLE.   Break Commandment Number One,
  And your ruin has begun.
  Break Commandment Number Two
  And the sky will lose its blue.
  Break Commandment Number Three
  And you dry the eternal sea.
  Break Commandment Number Four
  And the sun will rise no more.
  Break Commandment Number Five
  And your fields will never thrive.
  Break Commandment Number Six
  And the firmament unfix.
  Break Commandment Number Seven
  And you shut the road to Heaven.
  Break Commandment Number Eight
  And you lock the Heavenly Gate.
  Break Commandment Number Nine
  And the stars will cease to shine.
  Break Commandment Number Ten
  And you toll the doom of men.

    [*Throughout this rigmarole* JOEY *chimes in with :
    " Jump into the wind, Sir James," at regular
    intervals. It is growing to dusk. The clock chimes
    five.*

[23]

P.-P. Long, long ago, a friend of mine who had too
much money worked his way along Harley Street and
Wimpole Street, taking expert opinions about, I think, a
boil on his bottom. He got several admirable opinions,
all different. Indeed, they cancelled out. He took this as
an instruction that he should do nothing at all about the
boil, and it healed almost immediately.

BEADLE. Indeed? Most extraordinary! Well, it's
five o'clock and I don't think Lady Maggie can be coming.
So perhaps you'll excuse me.

JUDY. Of course. You must be very busy. It was
most good of you to come.

> [JUDY *and* POUNCE-PELLOTT *see* BEADLE *out, after he
> has shaken hands with* BABY *and nodded to* JOEY.

JOEY. Play the piano?

BABY. A bittie. Not much.

JOEY. We must play some duets.

BABY. I'm not good enough for that.

JOEY. I don't believe it. Let me see your hands. (*He
takes her hands.*) You're a pianist all right. You've got
the stretch. And the grip. Grip my hands. That's
right. And pads on the finger-tips. That's the sign.

BABY. Is it?

JOEY (*looking into her eyes*). Yes.

BABY. I can't bear practising.

JOEY. Nobody practises nowadays. You've got to
express yourself nowadays. You can't express yourself in
five finger exercises.

BABY. I don't know that I've got anything to express.

JOEY. That's because you're not awake yet. Your
eyes are puppy-shut.

BABY. Are they?

JOEY. Well, they're just open. You've got plenty to
express. You wait. Are we to be friends?

BABY. I suppose so, if you like.

JOEY. Good. We'll go for a walk tonight if it's not

[24]

raining.   Half-past eight at the Town Hall.   Best thing in the world for a hangover.

BABY.   You esteem yourself so as to be a fast worker, don't you ?

JOEY.   I have my moments.

[*Re-enter* JUDY *and* POUNCE-PELLOTT.

I must go now, too.   I wanted to give His Reverence a start.

JUDY.   Must you ?

JOEY.   Yes.   Bye-bye for now.   Bye-bye for now, Miss Baby.   Remember what I told you.

[*Exeunt* JOEY *and* POUNCE-PELLOTT.

JUDY.   What a nasty, common little man !

BABY.   Yes, he is, isn't he ?

JUDY.   Are you feeling better, darling ?

BABY.   Much better, thank you.

[*She drifts to the window and looks out.*   JUDY *gathers the tea-things.   Re-enter* POUNCE-PELLOTT.

JUDY.   Oh, my God ! . . . Did you *arrange* for those dreadful people to come here ?

P.-P.   No, darling.

JUDY.   Somebody or something must have arranged it. It was too *malignant* not to be done on purpose.

P.-P.   I liked them.   You must remember, it's all bound to be a little strange.   We must learn to adapt ourselves. You see, in a way it's a . . .

JUDY.   I know.   A new kind of world.   There's nothing very new about that lot.

P.-P.   No.   But the point is, they've learned to adapt themselves.   We've got to learn that, too, or we'll be blue with bruises.

[*Enter* TOBY, *a good imitation of* KETCH—*cap on head and cigarette in mouth.*

What do you want ?

[25]

TOBY.   You left the door open, so I came in.   Did you see a soldering bolt about ?

P.-P.   No.   And don't you take your hat off when you come into a room ?

TOBY (*cheekily*).   No, I don't, as a matter of fact.

P.-P. (*in a terrible voice*).   Jao !   Jaldi, soor ka batcha !

[TOBY *flees in terror*.

Is that the man you were talking about—the plumber ?

JUDY.   No.   That's the apprentice.

P.-P.   Oh ?

[*He relapses again into thought*.

JUDY.   Perhaps the old-fashioned way of talking is the best after all.   I wish you had been here when that man was here.   Baby, darling, do you feel fit enough to take this tray ?

BABY.   Yes, Mummy.

[BABY *takes the tray out*.

JUDY (*laughing*.)   You gave him a fright, poor little brute.

P.-P.   Did I ?

JUDY.   He went white.   I thought he would burst into tears.

[*Knock on the door*.

Who's that ?   Come in.

[KETCH *enters.   His cap is in his hand.   His manners are dignified and courteous.   His eyes are blazing with rage*.

KETCH.   I hope you will pardon my intrusion, but my apprentice has just made a complaint to me.   He is very much upset.   He entered your house on a perfectly legitimate errand, and was met by a torrent of foul language and abuse.

[26]

JUDY.   Your apprentice marched in here as bold as brass . . .

P.-P.   Wait a minute.   You're not Mr. Ketch, are you ?

KETCH.   That's me.

P.-P.   Don't you remember me ?

KETCH.   Your face seems sort of familiar.

P.-P.   Do you remember a child who fell overboard— from the *Brahmapootra* ?

KETCH (*surprised and embarrassed*).   God, yes.   That's funny, isn't it ?   You know, I'd forgotten your name. I've been through a lot since then, if you understand.

P.-P.   By Jove, what a piece of luck !   Come in.   Sit down.   Have a drink.   Judy, this is the man who jumped in after Baby.

[*He shakes* KETCH *warmly by the hand, and guides him to a chair.*

KETCH.   Ugh, it was naething.

P.-P.   My wife never saw you.   She was badly knocked up by the whole thing, of course.   She still won't talk about it.   And then, you were so damned elusive.   Well, well.   What will you have ?

KETCH.   I never touch it.

P.-P.   Have a cheroot, then.

KETCH.   All right.   Thanks.

P.-P.   Isn't that extraordinary, darling ?

JUDY.   Yes. . . . I . . . Mr. Ketch, I mean, I'm sorry . . . I don't know what to say. . . . Please forgive me. I'm an awful fool.

[*She hurries from the room.*

KETCH.   A bit emotional ?

P.-P.   It's not surprising.   I'll not go after her.   She'll cry for a bit, and then come back.   Our girl's quite grown up now.

KETCH.   That would be her I saw a wee while ago ?

P.-P.   Did you ?   I don't suppose you would recognise

[27]

her. Let me see. She would be about three years old. Fifteen years ago. Well, well.

KETCH. They change a lot in that time.

P.-P. Yes. Don't they? I must fetch her. She must thank you herself.

KETCH. No, no. Honest, another time. I'm not used to this kind of thing.

P.-P. Just as you wish. . . . What have you been doing with yourself all these years?

KETCH. It's a long story.

P.-P. Of course it is. You must forgive me for asking idiotic questions. It's not a very usual situation, is it? But we're neighbours now. We'll have plenty of time to pick up the threads.

KETCH. Maybe.

P.-P. No maybe about it. I'm not going to let you slip through my fingers again.

KETCH. I don't know about that. You see, I have certain principles.

P.-P. We all have, haven't we? What are your principles?

KETCH. I'm a Communist, for one thing.

P.-P. Oh, are you? That's very interesting. I'm delighted. You're the only friend I've got who's a Communist.

KETCH. I think you're going a bit fast. I don't know about friend. I don't pick my friends among the so-called upper classes myself.

P.-P. A very irrelevant remark. I'm a stranger here, but I had the impression that you had abolished all that.

KETCH. Abolished all what?

P.-P. Classes.

KETCH. That's where you're wrong. The class war hasna begun yet.

P.-P. You must tell me all about that. I'm a new boy. I'm beginning all over again. I was just telling Doctor Beadle. . . . Oh, there you are.

[28]

[*Enter* JUDY *and* BABY, *very solemn.*

JUDY. Baby, this is Mr. Ketch, who saved your life.
My daughter Cynthia, Mr. Ketch.

BABY. How do you do, and thank you very much for
saving my life.

KETCH. Don't mention it.   Anybody would have done
the same.

BABY. No. I don't remember anything about it, but it
must have been a very brave act.

JUDY. It was. It was. Oh, Mr. Ketch, I don't know
how to tell you how grateful we are to you.

KETCH. Ugh, forget it. It's time I was stepping. I
think your electric fire'll haud thegither for another week
or so, and thanks for the cheroot.

JUDY. No, no. You mustn't go yet.

KETCH. I've my work to do.

JUDY. But not after five o'clock. You'll wait for
dinner.

KETCH. No, thank you. My tea's waiting for me.
Me and the lad was just passing. You didna see a spanner,
did you ?

JUDY. No. You must have left it somewhere else.

KETCH. Maybe so. Well, cheerybye. . . . You're
looking none the worse of your accident, Miss.

BABY. No. I've quite recovered, thank you.

KETCH. That's good.

[*Bell rings.*

JUDY. Baby, the door.

[*Exit* BABY.

JUDY. Dear Baby. . . . Anything one can say is so
inadequate, Mr. Ketch . . .

KETCH. If it's a visitor, I'd better be getting out of
here.

P.-P. I don't think it can be. Sit down again for a
minute.

[29]

[*Enter* BABY *with* LADY MAGGIE REVENANT, *an incarnation of all that is vague.*

BABY.   Lady Maggie Revenant, Mummy.

JUDY.   Oh, how do you do?   You haven't met my husband—or Mr. Ketch.

LADY MAGGIE.   Oh, how do you do?   You were very kind to my brother in India, weren't you?   I should have called centuries earlier, but the time slipped by.

KETCH.   I'll away, then.

LADY MAGGIE.   Oh, are you going?   What a pity. Do look me up sometime, if you've nothing better to do. I'm rather a lonely sort of woman.   I could show you some awfully interesting water-colours by Princess Louise. She gave them to my sister on her tenth birthday.   But perhaps you're not interested in Art?

KETCH.   Well, I don't know much about it.

LADY MAGGIE.   Which of us does?   Well, good-bye. It's been delightful to meet you.

[*Exeunt* POUNCE-PELLOTT *and* KETCH.

JUDY.   Will you have some tea?

LADY MAGGIE.   No, I don't think so.   No.

JUDY.   Well, a glass of sherry, or something.

LADY MAGGIE.   Oh, no.   If I take a little, it does no good; and if I take a lot, it makes me so sad.   I weep, and things. . . . Oh, there's little Buddha.   It's astonishing how little character he has in his face, considering how influential he must have been.   A nice place you have here.

JUDY.   I don't like it very much.   But it was all we could afford—more than we could afford.   I'm afraid we were horribly swindled.

LADY MAGGIE.   Yes.   One is, isn't one?   If I buy anything it costs millions, and if I sell anything I get next to nothing.   Somebody, somewhere, must be doing very well.   It's a comforting thought.

JUDY.   You must have a nice nature if it comforts you.

LADY MAGGIE. I *have* a very nice nature. At least, Mr. Baldwin told me I had. I forget what we were talking about.

JUDY. Did you know Mr. Baldwin well?

LADY MAGGIE. Not well. . . . It's very pleasant to look out on the sea. Except when it shows its teeth. Do you like the sea?

JUDY. Not very much, I'm afraid.

LADY MAGGIE. I went round the world once. Mr. Bernard Shaw was on the ship.

JUDY. That must have been very interesting.

LADY MAGGIE. Yes. He had such a pretty white beard. It wagged when he talked. Where has your husband gone? He was very kind to my brother. Do you know the Arbuthnots?

JUDY. No, I don't think so.

LADY MAGGIE. Yes. I forgot. It was Jamaica they used to govern. I didn't like them much. Well, good-bye. I must be going, I think. You and your husband must come to see me. And we must have a long, long talk. You come, too, my dear, won't you?

BABY. Yes, thank you.

LADY MAGGIE. You're rather like Lydia Smith. But she was older. And she had rather a bad-tempered expression, poor thing. Her father was very bad-tempered. He hunted a good deal. His red face clashed horribly with his pink coat, I remember. But he's dead now. Practically everybody is dead, aren't they? Good-bye.

[*She drifts out, followed by* JUDY.

[*It is growing quite dark.* BABY *goes to the piano and plays with great energy and confidence, but little accuracy, some nasty thing like Saint-Saëns's* Danse Macabre. *This is shortly picked up by two more competent pianists, who play it through a black-out and the fall of the curtain.*

[31]

[*The Curtain falls to denote the passing of six hours.*

[*When it rises again,* P.-P. *switches on a standard lamp and is seen in his pyjamas and a dressing-gown.*

JUDY (*off*).   What is it, dear?

P.-P.   I'm looking for that Blue Book.

JUDY (*off*).   Ulysses?

P.-P.   No, no.   That Government thing on open-cast coal.

JUDY (*off*).   Baby isn't in yet.

P.-P.   Oh, isn't she?   I'd better wait up for her for a little.

JUDY (*off*).   Put the fire on, then, and don't catch cold.

P.-P.   Righto.

[*Switches on the fire, pulls a sofa under the lamp and settles down to read.*

JUDY (*off*).   Don't be long.   Good-night.

P.-P.   Good-night, darling.

[*The wind howls and the lights begin to dim and go blue. The door opens gradually of itself.   Soon the room is lit only by moonlight.* POTHECARY *comes in, carrying a Hand of Glory with green lights at the finger-tips. She is fantastically dressed, with a hint of the mediæval leech about her.   She carries a jar of leeches in her free hand.   She is followed by* LADY MAGGIE, *looking much as she did on her last appearance, and by a strange* WOMAN *with an American accent and a sugar-loaf hat.   This is a projection of* JEMIMA LEE CROWE, *who is to appear later.*

POTHECARY.   Sleep those that sleep.   Wake those that wake.

Be as the deid, for Satan's sake.

LADY MAGGIE.   We have a new sister.

POTHECARY.   Don't name her name.

LADY MAGGIE.   She is from Virginia.   A long way.

JEMIMA. I bring you sororial greetings from the
Alpha Beta Phi Coven of Stubbs, Spottsville. May I be
allowed to express the pleasure I feel in . . .

POTHECARY. Not yet.

LADY MAGGIE. What have you got in your wee jam-
pot ?

POTHECARY. Leeches, Cummer. Leeches for the belted
    Knight.
    Wee, hungry sucking leeches. Wheesht.

[*The three whisper.*

LADY MAGGIE. The grey howlet has three times
    whooed.
    The grinning cat has three times mewed.
    The tod has yowled three times in the wood
    At the red mune cowering ahint the cloud.

POTHECARY. Cummer, go ye afore. Cummer gae ye.
    Gin ye winna gang afore, Cummer, let me.
    Linkin, linkin widdershins,
    Ring-a-ring a-widdershins,
    Cummers, carline, crone and queyn,
    Round gae we.

[*Slow dance to this rhyme.*

JEMIMA. Have you an Officer to the Coven ?

LADY MAGGIE. Aye, Joey Mascara by name.

POTHECARY. Joey's coming. . . . And Yon Yin's
coming.

JEMIMA. Who's Yon Yin ?

POTHECARY. Wheesht !

[*Silence and stillness, during which the shadow of a huge
    black dog progresses round the flats.*

It's Yon Yin.

LADY MAGGIE. Yon Yin.

JEMIMA. O Satan, preserve us. O Satan, guide us.
O Satan, swing over us thy black, black wings.

D   [33]

[JOEY, *disguised as a Harlequinade Clown, leaps into the room.*

JOEY.   Houp-la, here we are again !
POTHECARY.   Is it you, Officer ?
JOEY.   Aye, Nickniven, it's me.   Are ye met, are ye set, ye black toad's get ?
LADY MAGGIE.   We're met and we're set.
JOEY.   Wha's the third ?
POTHECARY.   A delegate from over the salt water.
JOEY.   Pleased to meet you.
JEMIMA.   Happy to make your acquaintance, Officer.
LADY MAGGIE.   Is he coming ?
JOEY.   Aye, he's coming.
POTHECARY.   The sterns hae cruppen deep in the lift.
    Tear us a rift, cantrip, tear us a rift.
    Leerie licht the lamp wi' a brand frae Hell.
    Show us Himsel !
JOEY.   Rise up, foul fiend !

[*He beats the ground three times with his poker.   Black-
    out and Thunder.   THE DE'IL appears as a tall, black
    man in a frock coat with big white cuffs as a red light
    glows.   The dog's shadow crosses again.*

THE DE'IL.   Weel, Cummers, you're here.   I'm blythe to see ye, Cummers.   What hae ye for me the nicht ?
POTHECARY.   We've a Maiden for ye, Clootie.
LADY MAGGIE.   Aye, a Maiden.
POTHECARY.   Name us, quickly.   Name us.
JEMIMA.   First let me say, on behalf of the very ancient and honourable Coven of Stubbs, Spottsville, Virginia, what a very real pleasure and honour it is to take part in this highly memorable occasion.
THE DE'IL.   Not at all.   Not at all.
JEMIMA.   No, but you must allow me.   I am certain that I shall take back with me to my home town many happy memories of this delightful and epoch-making

occasion.   May I say that my pleasure would be enhanced
if I could take back with me a personal message from your
Infernal Excellency to my colleagues, the ladies of Stubbs ?
Our Coven is of quite respectable antiquity, going back,
as it does, to the days of the Puritan Fathers, and I assure
you they would esteem it a privilege to have you notify
them of your general and particular interest in their work.

THE DE'IL.   Tell them they're doing fine.   And now I
name thee Tiggerbricht . . . (*To* POTHECARY) . . . And
thee, Nickniven . . . (*To* LADY MAGGIE) . . . And thee,
Pickle-next-the-wind.

POTHECARY.   Ho !

LADY MAGGIE.   Ho !

JEMIMA.   Ho !

JOEY.   Ho, ho, ho !

OMNES (*dancing*).   Cummer, gang afore, Cummer, gang
ye.

　　Gin ye winna gae afore, Cummer, let me.

　　Tinkletum, tankletum,

　　Brinkletum, brankletum,

　　Ring, ring widdershins,

　　Round gae we.

　　　[THE DE'IL *pulls* JEMIMA *roughly from the ring.   She is
　　　delighted.*

THE DE'IL.   Whaur's your mark ?   Whaur was you
nippit ?

JEMIMA.   Here.

　　　　　　　　　　　　　　　　　[*Bares a shoulder.*

THE DE'IL.   Aye.   You're weel nippit.

　　　[*He kisses her violently and throws her to the ground.
　　　The* OTHERS *gather round to examine the mark.*

JEMIMA.   Well, I must say that was a very great honour.

THE DE'IL.   Get up.   Whaur's the Maiden ?

JOEY.   I'll get her.

[*Exit* JOEY.

[*The dance goes on.*

POTHECARY. A sermon. A sermon.

JEMIMA. Yes. Do let's have a sermon.

LADY MAGGIE. Quiet, everybody.

THE DE'IL. Queerly Beshoven : It bemoves me on this
jollem oblation to squeak a few worden on Graith, Rope
and Parity. How often hae we pled wi' oorselves, " Gaby,
it's shark ootside " and failed to find in our scart of scarts
a sausage factory co-respondence ? Nae answer. The
cauld crivens are silos. What for ? Whertofore ? I'll
explicate. Ye've shooned in on the wrang stave-length, wi'
your hosannahs, and your bananas, and your ballyhooyers.
I infer you to the words of the Profit-an-loss Poosienancie
whilk you will find in Chap at the Door, Verse Vica.
" Behold the waughwachterie of grooshallachie is abune
you. Selah."

JEMIMA. Glory. Glory.

POTHECARY. Hullaballooya.

THE DE'IL. But stay. I maun intervergiserate my
cobjurations. The Wee Yin approaches. To be skim-
bimbled in wur text. Amen.

[*Enter* JOEY *with* BABY. *She is dressed in white.*

JOEY. Here's the Maiden.

THE DE'IL. You're for joining us, my dear ?

BABY. Aye.

THE DE'IL. That's my dilly and my darling. Now, gin
you'll allow me a few moments to compose my thochts,
Nicniven, here, will tell you what there is to dae.

[THE DE'IL, JEMIMA, LADY MAGGIE *and* JOEY *go into a
kind of sinister huddle up stage.* POTHECARY *leads*
BABY *forward.*

POTHECARY. You're for turning a witch, my hen ?

BABY. Aye.

[36]

POTHECARY. Dinna be feart, then. This is what ye maun do. First, ye'll renounce your baptism.

BABY. I dinna remember a thing about my baptism. I was owre wee.

POTHECARY. A' the better. And your Faith.

BABY. I've nae faith in a' body.

POTHECARY. This is what you'll dae. You'll kick off your shoon and put a haun on the sole of your left foot, like this. And a haun on your croon, like this, and you'll say after the De'il what he tells you to say.

BABY. O.K.

POTHECARY. Then the De'il will give you a gey sair pinch in whatever place it pleases him to pinch you. It'll burn like Hell's flames for a minute, but syne he'll stroke it.

BABY. I know. I've been vaccinated.

POTHECARY. And syne the pain will go for ever and ever; for you'll hae the witches mark on you, and on that spot you'll feel naething, never no more. And you'll shed nae mair tears, e'en gin ye ettle to greet. And you'll have the power—Black Magic and White Magic—o'er things and folk, living and deid.

BABY. I'm sure that will be very nice.

POTHECARY. Are ye ready for 't ?

BABY. Aye.

POTHECARY (*to* THE DE'IL). She's a' preparit.

[*The* GROUP *at the back advances.*

THE DE'IL. Etherum, Petherum, Hinkiemajoke,
          Burn lowe, rise smoke.
     Come under the lintel o' the Everlasting Kingdom.

[POUNCE-PELLOTT *on his sofa gives a loud and terrible cry.*

What's that ?

POTHECARY. The Hand o' Glory's loweing low. We maun awa.

[*It suddenly grows very dark.   The Hand of Glory goes out.*

[THE DE'IL *vanishes with a " hollow and ghoustie " moan.*

JEMIMA.   This is very, very awkward.

LADY MAGGIE.   There's no time to lose.   Quick !

POTHECARY.   Horse and hattock, in the Divell's name.

JOEY (*bellowing*).   Horse and hattock, horse and go.

OMNES.   Horse and hattock ! ! !   Harness the wind to the ragwort coaches.   Horse and hattock !

[*Confusion.   Black-out.*

P.-P.   Wake up.   Wake up.   In the name of the Father, the Son, and the Holy Ghost.   The switch.   The switch. Where's the . . . Oh !

[*The lights go up.*   P.-P. *is alone.*

P.-P.   Cheese pudding.   Damn that cheese pudding. . . Oh dear.   I must have dropped over.

[*A door bangs and a key turns.*

Is that you, darling ?

BABY (*off*).   Yes, Daddy.

P.-P.   I'm in the parlour.

BABY (*off*).   I'm practically dead.   I'll go to bed, if you don't mind.   I've locked the door.

P.-P.   All right.   Good-night, lovey.

BABY.   Good-night, Daddy.   Happy dreams.

[POUNCE-PELLOTT *switches out the fire.*

CURTAIN

ACT II

The same, five days later.

> [JUDY, *in overalls, is dusting. The door slams. She listens. Muffled voices. The word " geography " is heard. Shortly after, enter* POUNCE-PELLOTT, *full of beans.*

P.-P. By Jove ! What a day. It's like June.

JUDY. Like Hell, you mean.

P.-P. The sea's like a millpond. I saw a dozen divers diving their little souls out. And you'll never guess who I met.

JUDY. I shan't try. I'm too busy.

P.-P. Copper.

JUDY. What ?

P.-P. Don't you remember ? He was Assistant Provost Marshal with that brigade that came up to Junglipore in '42 or '43. A ranker. A most amusing chap.

JUDY. Oh, that horrible fellow ! He got rather drunk.

P.-P. Only once. And he's awfully respectable now. He's some sort of controller for the Ministry of Interference. A Civil Servant, like me.

JUDY. Is he ?

P.-P. I've brought him in for a drink.

JUDY. You've what ?

P.-P. Yes. He said he could take a few minutes off.

JUDY. Very kind of him. At eleven o'clock on my busiest morning, with Baby away at the typewriting college and the char laid up with rheumatics and your ridiculous dinner-party tonight. Where is this man ?

P.-P. Washing his hands. And there's another thing.

JUDY. Oh, Lord, what ?

[39]

P.-P.   I've had a wire from Mrs. Crowe.   I picked it up from the telegraph boy.

JUDY.   Mrs. Crowe?

P.-P.   *You* know.   The American publisher woman. She's driving down this morning.

JUDY.   Dearest, we're not at Junglipore now, you know. Look at me.   *I* am your sole establishment.   We haven't got forty servants, here, in Baikie.

P.-P.   We can lunch at the Hotel.

JUDY.   Oh yes, we can lunch at the Hotel.   Here, let me get out of this.

> [*As she reaches the door,* COPPER *comes in—a rather dull-looking, pompous man in his fifties.*

COPPER.   Good morning, Lady Pellott.   Do you remember me?

JUDY.   Of course I do, Captain Copper.   How do you do?   What in the world are you doing here?

COPPER.   I met your good man and he asked me in for old time's sake.   It's a small world, isn't it?

JUDY.   Microscopic.

P.-P.   Copper's a burra-wallah here now.   Most important chap.   You'd better be polite to him.

JUDY.   Yes, I realise that. . . . Would you think me most awfully rude, Captain Copper, if I went on with my housework?

COPPER.   Not at all.

JUDY.   Things aren't quite the same as they used to be.

COPPER.   Changed days.   Changed days.

JUDY.   Yes.   So, if you'll excuse me . . . Polly, when is that terrible woman coming?

P.-P.   I don't think she's necessarily going to be terrible.

JUDY.   Yes, she is.   Like an army with banners.   I want to know when to expect this act of aggression.

P.-P. (*looking at telegram*).   " Dear Sir James I am hiring an automobile and expect God willing to arrive at your hospitable home sometime in the neighbourhood of high noon trusting that you and her ladyship are in good health with the warmest esteem and regards jemima lee crowe."

COPPER. Some telegram !

JUDY. Some invasion. Oh, good Lord, I must run.

[*Exit* JUDY.   P.-P. *prepares drinks.*

P.-P.   Pink ?

COPPER.   Much obliged.

P.-P.   She's quite an important lady, this.   She's one of the partners in Crowe and Van Houten, the Boston publishers.   I can't imagine what she wants with me.

COPPER.   If she brings some dollars into the country, it will be all to the good.   Thank you.   Best respects. We need all the hard currency we can get these days, I may tell you confidentially.   Keep it under your hat.

P.-P.   Yes, I will.   I'm sure you're right.

COPPER.   I don't make many mistakes.

P.-P.   Would you like to meet her ?

COPPER.   Well, I only dropped in for a minute.   The work of the country's got to go on, you know; and if she's not coming till twelve . . .

P.-P.   You'd better come to dinner tonight.   We've two or three people coming in.   It's to be a sort of symposium, and it would be most valuable to have somebody who could talk with authority.

COPPER.   I'm afraid I'm not much in the talking line. You know, we're known as the silent service.

P.-P.   I thought that was the Navy.

COPPER.   It used to be, I believe.   It's the Civil Service now.

P.-P.   You can keep us on the right lines, anyhow.

COPPER.   Oh, I can do that, all right. . . . What's this sym—what-do-you-call-it about ?

P.-P.   It's to help me, really.   You see, I'm starting all over again from scratch.

COPPER.   I don't see why you should, with your experience.   If anybody knows how to push people about, you
should.

P.-P.   But life's not all pushing people about.

COPPER.   Most of it is.

P.-P.   But, even if it were, you've got to know where to
push them.

COPPER.   That's immaterial.   " Keep 'em moving ";
that's the good old police motto.

P.-P.   I see.

COPPER (*getting up*).   Well, that's what the doctor
ordered.   It's time I was getting back to the office.

P.-P.   You'll come to dinner ?   Half-past seven.   Don't
dress.

COPPER.   Well, it's very kind of you, but . . .

P.-P.   Lady Pellott will take no denial.   She'll be heart-
broken if you don't come.

COPPER.   Well, if you put it that way . . .

P.-P.   Good.

> [*They go out.   In a moment* JUDY *comes in* (*overalls off*),
> *puts back the gin and straightens the room.   She is in a
> rage.   Re-enter* POUNCE-PELLOTT.

JUDY.   You bat-witted, irresponsible, damned swine !

P.-P.   Why ?   What's the matter, darling ?

JUDY.   I heard you.   I heard you ask that brute to
dinner.

P.-P.   Yes.   I did, as a matter of fact.   I'm terribly
anxious to get his angle.   You see . . .

JUDY.   And this Yankee m-m-m-monstress will no
doubt be staying, too ?

P.-P.   Well, I don't know what her plans are, but . . .

JUDY.   I'm going straight away to put my head in the
gas oven.

P.-P.   That's surely rather drastic.

JUDY.   It isn't.   Life's not worth living.

P.-P.   How do you know ?   We've got to give this new kind of life a fair trial.   We . . .

JUDY.   Shut up !! . . . I don't think you're a bit funny.   I think all this stuff of yours is a very disagreeable pose, and not funny in the slightest degree.   And even if it were, it's no excuse for torturing your wife and driving her mad, do you hear ?   I can't bear it.   As if Baby weren't enough to worry the soul out of anybody.

P.-P.   Baby's all right.

JUDY.   She's not all right, and you know it.

P.-P.   She'll steady up.   She's at a difficult age.

JUDY.   Why don't you speak to her ?

P.-P.   I do speak to her.

JUDY.   You know perfectly well what I mean.

P.-P.   I'm not going to make an enemy of my own child.

JUDY.   Would you rather she went on the streets ? She's practically there already.

P.-P.   Oh, nonsense !

JUDY.   The char's niece saw her at that filthy Spa, dancing with your disgusting friend Mascara.

P.-P.   Mascara's a very intelligent little chap.   She could learn quite a lot from him.

JUDY.   I should just think she could !

P.-P.   It's no fun working all day at a typewriting school.   Young people have got to have some outlet. And they're far better to find their way about for themselves.   Especially when you and I don't know our way about.

JUDY.   All right.   Have it your own way.   You seem to want to make my house a dump for all the rag-tag and bobtail of this midden of a place.   You may as well make it a crèche for your little bastard grandchildren.

P.-P.   Darling, pull yourself together.   I know it's tough for you, getting used to all this.   But we've got to take our ups with our downs and I suppose, in the long run, it's good for the soul.

[43]

JUDY.   And don't be so bloody tender.   I can't bear it,
I tell you, I can't bear it.   I'm getting out of this.   I'm
going now to pack.   You can entertain your own blasted
friends.

P.-P.   Judy, don't talk rot.

JUDY.   Damn you, I'm not going to talk to you at all.
Ever again.   I was at breaking-point long ago.   This is
the finish.   I hope you understand that.   I'm leaving you,
do you understand ?   Get that into your thick head, you
idle, conceited fool.   Get it well in.   Because I mean what
I say.

[*Bell rings.*

JUDY.   Oh, what's this now ?
P.-P.   I'll go.

> [*Exit* P.-P.   JUDY *gives herself a rub down.   Voices in
> the lobby.   Re-enter* P.-P. *with a highly spectacular*
> MRS. JEMIMA LEE CROWE.

P.-P.   Judy, this is Mrs. Crowe.

JUDY.   How do you do ?

JEMIMA.   How do you do, Lady Pounce-Pellott.   I am
really most happy to make your acquaintance.   Indeed, I
couldn't wait till I had come right down to satisfy my
curiosity about you and your celebrated husband.   And
what a nice little dwelling you have here !   Right on the
edge of the ocean.   My, my.   I wish my Halbert had
been with me for all this.   But he's passed on, you see.
I'm a widow.

JUDY.   I'm so sorry.

JEMIMA.   Don't mention it.   Don't mention it at all.
It is some years since Halbert was taken away, and time
is a great healer of heartbreak.   I hope you may never,
never have to experience that fact, Lady Pounce-Pellott;
but, at the same time, you may take it from me that it is
perfectly accurate.   I thought I should never get over my
sad loss; but here I am.

[44]

JUDY. Well, now, that's very nice.

JEMIMA. I take great consolation out of our little business. When Halbert departed I just dried my eyes and rolled up my sleeves and took up his work where he left it. Last year we turned over pretty nearly two million dollars.

JUDY. That must have been a great comfort.

JEMIMA. You've said it.

P.-P. Two million dollars. Well, well.

JEMIMA. But it may not surprise you to learn, Sir James, that I didn't make that only by talking about the weather. I can't help it. The Almighty made me that way, I reckon; but I am a woman of action. I always think that action speaks a long way louder than words, and I always say, " Give me action, every time; polite conversation afterwards." I can't help it, Lady Pounce-Pellott, but that's how I'm made. So, if you'll very kindly be lenient with my idiosyncracies, I should like to, as we say in the States, talk turkey and talk it good.

JUDY. Why, certainly, if you'd like to.

JEMIMA. I'd like to very much. And it is most courteous of you, and only what I should expect from you, that you give me the necessary permission. Sir James, I have come all this way to see you with a certain proposition.

P.-P. Oh ?

JEMIMA. Does the name Elmer J. F. X. Rosenbaum convey anything to you ?

P.-P. Yes. He's a journalist, isn't he ? He came to see us at Junglipore. Nice fellow.

JEMIMA. He is one of my dearest friends. It is a purely platonic friendship, because some years ago I decided to cut sexual relationships clean out of my life. I felt that I had a mission, and that sexual relationships were apt to be irrelevant and a liability to a woman with a mission. You must be aware of this from the histories of your own Florence Nightingale and Elizabeth Fry. So I said to Elmer, " Please. Let us understand one another. Sensuality is right out." So he said he would be a good

[45]

boy and, you will be pleased to learn, he has kept his promise—meticulously. Ah, well!

JUDY.   Would you like a cup of tea, or a drink, or anything?

JEMIMA.   No, my dear, thank you.   In some ways I flatter myself I am more English than the English, but I have *never* habituated myself to tea-drinking.   I can't help it.   It's the way I'm made.   And if folks can't take me the way I am, all I can say is, " I'm sorry.   I can't help it."

P.-P.   A drink, then?

JEMIMA.   Not at this time in the morning and while we are talking business.   Sir James, my Incorporation has enpowered me to offer you seven thousand dollars on account of royalties for the World rights of your Indian reminiscences.

P.-P.   But . . . I mean to say . . .

JEMIMA.   No.   I quite understand.   You must have time to think it over.   In girlhood I used to be blamed for rushing my male acquaintances off their feet; but I'm not that sort of a girl now.   You can have plenty of time.

P.-P.   But I've never had the slightest intention of writing my . . .

JUDY.   I wonder whether we couldn't discuss it better on a basis of ten thousand dollars.

JEMIMA.   Now, there speaks the hard-headed woman of affairs.   Well, you know what I mean by affairs.   I use the word in no derogatory sense.   Well, Lady Pounce-Pellott, it is a very valuable thing to have a sound basis of discussion.   If you and your husband are prepared to talk on the basis of ten thousand dollars, it would be a thousand pities to put any obstacles in your way.

P.-P.   What did this fellow—Rosenbaum—say to you?

JEMIMA.   Elmer?   Mind, I want it to be perfectly clear that I am not permitting myself to be unduly influenced by the peculiar relations in which Elmer and I stand to each other.   If you desire proof of my entire objectivity,

I may say that Elmer has more than once proposed
marriage to me. But I said, " No. I must think of
Halbert. In his bodily phase, he was a very, very impul-
sive person. There are no black eyes in heaven, Elmer," I
said, " but woe to him by whom the offence cometh; and
I've no desire to start anything there," I said. Elmer
has a very high regard for your capabilities, Sir James.
He said you were the only one among all the stuffed shirts
in Hindustan who had an authentic angle on the situation.
He formed the opinion that the unloading of the Indian
Empire was a very, very significant occasion, and that it
would be highly informing to our several million readers
to have an authoritative person give them the low down
on it. So here I am, with ten thousand dollars down and
plenty more to come.

JUDY. How much more?

JEMIMA. Let me see. Naturally we should make a
feature of it. At a venture, I should say about 120,000
dollars while the sales last, apart from movie and radio and
television rights. Let us say, on a conservative estimate,
200,000 dollars.

JUDY. That's thirty thousand pounds.

JEMIMA. Thereabouts.

JUDY. Thank you.

JEMIMA. It's a pleasure.

JUDY. Do you mind if we go to the Hotel for lunch ?
It won't be a very good lunch, I'm afraid.

JEMIMA. Oh, my dear, you don't need to tell me anything about that. It is thoroughly realised how the
British Islands have suffered by assisting us to salvage
civilisation.

JUDY. Then we're having a little dinner-party tonight.
You might be amused. We're having quite a little cross-
section of Scottish life. Odd people, but they might
interest you.

JEMIMA. An initial difficulty is that my glad rags are
way back in the city.

[47]

JUDY. Oh, we're not dressing up. It's absolutely informal.

JEMIMA. Well, now, isn't that sweet ? Of all things in the world, I like informality the best. I'll be most happy to come to your little party, Lady Pounce-Pellott . . . and, in the meanwhile . . .

[*She rummages in her handbag.*

P.-P. Oh, I'm so sorry. Will you have a cigarette ?

JEMIMA. If you'll forgive me, I'll have one of my own. They have a certain kick. Perhaps you'll excuse me for observing that that is what we Americans miss most over here. In your food, in your drinks, in your plays, in your noospapers, you seem to lack a kick.

[*As she continues rummaging, a rather heavy revolver drops on the floor.*

[P.-P. *gives it to her.*

Ah, thank you. That's my little gun.

P.-P. Do you always carry a gun ?

JEMIMA. Yes. I feel more confident that way. I like to know that my jools and my virtue and what you would call my way of living are safe. I'm rather a nervous sort of girl, and not adventurous, not deep down within me. Do you think that funny in a descendant of the Pilgrim Fathers ? But, you see, I've got a Portuguese strain in me, too. . . . And now you must let me lay down the schedule for the day. You two put on your woolly coats and scarves, and I'll take you for a nice ride into the mountains.

JUDY. Oh, Mrs. Crowe, I couldn't. I've got that dinner to get ready.

JEMIMA. An hour or two of pure fresh air won't hurt you. And you, Sir James ?

P.-P. I'm terribly sorry I can't. I've—well—I've got to see my doctor in a few minutes.

JEMIMA. Are you sick ?

[48]

P.-P.   No.   But I've got into the habit of having an overhaul.

JEMIMA.   Very well.   Very wise.   Now, Lady Pounce-Pellott, go and get your wraps.

JUDY.   I oughtn't to.

JEMIMA.   A very, very good female reason for doing it.

JUDY.   I shan't be a minute.

[*Exit* JUDY.

P.-P.   This is really most awfully good of you.

JEMIMA.   You have such a strong face, Sir James.   The typical pro-consul.   There is sadness in it, too.   I should not be surprised if women fall for you in a big way.

P.-P.   I'm afraid they don't. . . . But, about this book. I feel rather shattered.   I've never had the least idea of writing a book.   I doubt whether I could.

JEMIMA.   Elmer will look after the style.   You give him the goods, and he'll make them attractive.   We need say no more about that.

P.-P.   But nothing I could write about India could possibly interest anyone but a few of my friends.

JEMIMA.   Please.   The Decline and Fall of the British Empire is of stupendous general interest.   Anyway, I trust Elmer's hunches, specially when they are reinforced by my own.   Our little talk has quite convinced me that we have got something here.   So say no more.   I find you a very, very attractive person.

P.-P.   Naturally I'm delighted that you should.

JEMIMA.   I look forward to us getting together.

P.-P.   Oh, I mean to say, so do I.   But . . .

JEMIMA.   Tell me all about yourself.

P.-P.   That's rather a large order.

JEMIMA.   I deal exclusively in large orders.

[*Re-enter* JUDY, *all wrapped up.*

JUDY.   I say, what about lunch?

E   [49]

JEMIMA.   We'll find a roadhouse.

JUDY.   Can you manage, Polly ?

P.-P.   Perfectly well.

JUDY.   But we must be back in time to get the dinner ready.

JEMIMA.   If you can fit me out with a pinafore, I'll help you.   I am very, very domesticated.   And now you must show me your beautiful country.   Be as good as you can till I come back, dear Jim. . . . You don't mind me calling him Jim, Lady Pounce-Pellott ?

JUDY.   Not in the least.

JEMIMA.   That's fine.   You must call me Jemima. Elmer calls me Cuddles.   You can call me that if you like. Come right along.

[*Exeunt* JEMIMA *and* JUDY.

[P.-P., *in a state of heavily suppressed excitement, gets paper and a pencil and begins to do calculations.   In a reverie, he speaks :*

P.-P.   A thousand memories for export only.
They will rise, they will rise,
As the bright greenbacks flick the surface of the
dreaming, brown lochan.
Money, money, money, leap at it, my beauties.
You will be rich fish and your King Fish,
The Master of you all, will live happy ever after.

Memories for sale !
There's rosemary, on account, for remembrance ;
And what am I bid for a little bit of rue ?

What am I bid for the deodar and cherry
Beyond the Mutteeanee Pass, deep in the Himalayas ?
What am I bid for the mist on the Khyber,
And the dawn on the tombs of the Jains thrown in as
a bargain ?

[50]

I knew Rabindranath Tagore.   A decent fellow.
Nehru's a decent fellow too.
A bit Oxford and inclined to fiddle
While Bombay burns, like the ghats on the hill.
Smouldering fire.   Lord Curzon said to me . . .

How much for the purple buffaloes, the bushy-tailed
    tree rats,
And, God damn it, the clink of the tonga bar ?

" He is seeking the Way, a bairagi avowed."

When I was at Simla . . .

The dear smell of cedar, my darling brown people,
Moving, dreamily, nowhere . . .

O Karma . . . Om mane padme hum . . .

Cream coloured blossoms and tangled lianas,
Sambhurs breaking the bamboo thicket.
Trumpets and elephants and cloth of gold.

Trumpets and cloth of gold . . .
Gold . . . gold . . . gold . . .

I will sell you my memories, honey,
Honey-honey . . . honey . . .
So cloying and yellow, like gold . . .
Gilt-edged, golden-bodied Security . . .
(St. Louis Woman, with your diamond ring) . . .
" And the karela, the bitter karela shall cover it all."

                                        [*The bell rings.*

Damn . . .

          [*He goes out and presently leads in* DR. POTHECARY, *who
          throws her hat on a chair, her coat on a sofa, and
          herself on the hearth-rug.   She then sighs deeply.*

What's the matter ?

                    [51]

POTHECARY. Nothing's the matter. I'm all in. Damn this bloody National Health Act.

P.-P. Would you like a drink?

POTHECARY. No. I get amorous when I drink. I mustn't be that. I must be strictly professional.

[*She covers up her legs.*

P.-P. Of course.

POTHECARY. One thing the Health Act's done. It's discovered a new pleasure for the masses. The delight of being ill. I wish I could be ill. A sick woman's a Queen in Babylon, and all the rest are Christian slaves. Gosh, I'm tired. And I've still got twenty-five visits to do.

P.-P. You'd better have a drink.

POTHECARY. I told you. Can I trust you?

P.-P. (*getting drink*). I haven't the faintest idea.

POTHECARY. Haven't you? Righto . . . (*she gets up*). Now what's the matter with you?

P.-P. (*handing drink*). I have headaches.

POTHECARY. What sort of headaches?

P.-P. Heavy headaches. Pressing down that way. (*He presses his hand down on his head*). I still get a malarial rigor, now and again.

POTHECARY. Yes. Lie down on the sofa and loosen your waistcoat and shirt.

[P.-P. *obeys.*

You looked a bit hyper-manic when you opened the door to me.

P.-P. What's hyper-manic?

POTHECARY. Cerebrally excited. Raised.

[*She listens to him with a stethoscope, taps his knees, etc., during the dialogue.*

P.-P. I had had good news. Or what you might call good news.

[52]

POTHECARY.   Where's Lady Pellott?

P.-P.   Gone out with the good news.

POTHECARY.   How do you get on with her?

P.-P.   Fine.

POTHECARY.   It's not that that's worrying you, then?

P.-P.   Oh, not a bit.

POTHECARY.   Then you're worried about the child.

P.-P.   Yes . . . you see, it doesn't matter about me and
Judy.   It's rather fun for us, and we shall both be out of it
in a very few years' time.   But there's nowhere to put our
egg, if you see what I mean.   Everything is in such a
mess.   Within broad limits I don't give a hoot what kind
of society she fits into, so long as it's some kind of society,
but there seems to be no order and no place and nothing
but a milling crowd shouting paranoid doctrines out of a
whirlpool.

POTHECARY.   There's a lot in what you say.

P.-P.   I can't find a nest, if you see what I mean, or
anywhere to put it.

POTHECARY.   If people would only listen to the
scientists.

P.-P.   What would they be told if they listened?

POTHECARY.   Well, I'm a bit biased.   I'm a B.Sc. in
pure science as well as an M.B., Ch.B., but it all seems so
simple to us.   Society is an organism, like anything else;
and here we have a number of people who know something about organisms—how they organise themselves
and how to organise them to make them do what we want.
Yet, does anyone think of letting us boss the show?   Do
they hell!   All our work has to be filtered through
damned little committees of amateurs who haven't the
faintest idea what they are talking about.   If you sacked
the Cabinet and put in the Royal Society for ten years
you'd be surprised how things would straighten out.

P.-P.   I see.   It's all chemistry, isn't it?

POTHECARY.   Of course it's all chemistry—and bio-
physics.

E 2   [53]

P.-P.   What about the immortal soul ?

POTHECARY.   We've got the tabs on that too, thanks to Freud.

P.-P.   The tabs, eh ?

POTHECARY.   Well, damn it, you've got to know what you're dealing with.

P.-P.   I see.   When, say, a Mr. McGuire approaches me in the street with the idea of tapping me on the head with a cosh and improving his economic circumstances by taking my pocket-book, it is most valuable to know not only all about economics, but that Mr. McGuire is a remarkable anatomical and physiological machine composed of a peculiar arrangement of electrons and protons and occupying space by virtue of certain co-relating circumstances which are not yet completely understood.   It would be very interesting to wake up from one's unconscious state after the inevitable had happened and to speculate on the nature of consciousness . . .

POTHECARY.   If you're not going to be serious, I'd better push off.

P.-P.   It is only fair to science to say that it might have had the decency to supply me with a knuckleduster and information as to the correct place to hit Mr. McGuire.

POTHECARY.   If you give science a chance at Mr. McGuire, we'll deal with him all right.

P.-P.   I doubt it very much.   Science appears to me to be doing its best to save Mr. McGuire from one of its own excellent inventions—the six-foot drop ; with the sole result that we have plenty of exciting murders to read about in the Sunday papers.

POTHECARY.   That's because you've never given us a chance.

P.-P.   Nonsense.   Science has only got to whisper, and the whole of mankind flings itself on its face and beats the ground with its brow.   Most of us are quite prepared to walk into your laboratory cages and be nice, biddable guinea-pigs for you. You show your gratitude by inventing methods for our destruction.

POTHECARY. But we don't *control* them.

P.-P. If you can't control the infernal stuff that you make yourselves, then I'm damned if I'll let you control me.

POTHECARY. Do you know, I rather think you are a psychopathic personality. You may not know it, but you've got a suicide impulse due to strongly repressed aggression—with a touch of the incest motive as a make-weight.

P.-P. But, surely . . .

POTHECARY. No. Not another word. The consultation's over. . . . How are you liking Baikie?

P.-P. Well, I'm not quite orientated yet; but it seems all right.

POTHECARY. That's quite right. I don't think you *are* completely orientated.

P.-P. How long have you been in Baikie?

POTHECARY. Years and years. How old would you say I was?

P.-P. It's impossible to say whether you are late summer or early autumn.

POTHECARY. That's rather pretty. I'm afraid I should be very careful with you, Sir James.

P.-P. I only said how you appeared to me. I think you told me to be perfectly frank.

POTHECARY. Did I?

P.-P. I think so.

POTHECARY. I've been psychoanalysed twice, you must remember.

P.-P. Why should I remember that?

POTHECARY. One of the minor points about it is that we have all our motives and instincts under observation.

P.-P. They must be a fascinating sight.

POTHECARY. So it's no use paying compliments to the likes of me.

[55]

P.-P. If I may pay you one compliment, may I say that I never supposed it was.

POTHECARY. Thank you. I appreciate that. (*She looks at him meditatively.*) You're the sort of man we like to help.

P.-P. Oh?

POTHECARY. Yes.

P.-P. You say "we." Is this a sort of collective impulse?

POTHECARY. I'll say "I" if you like.

P.-P. That's much better. I like it better that way. And I want your help.

POTHECARY. Good. I should be going now.

P.-P. Oh, must you? My wife won't be home for lunch, and we might share a tin of sardines.

POTHECARY. Good heavens, man, I'm coming to dinner tonight . . . quite apart from the fact that I've got my work to do.

P.-P. But this is your work . . . doing good. Healing the sick.

POTHECARY. I'm afraid you're a bit of a philanderer, do you know?

P.-P. I wish I were. I can think of no more delightful hobby. . . . No, I'm a lost child. I'm appealing entirely to your maternal instinct.

POTHECARY. What is this dinner-party tonight? What is it for?

P.-P. I told you what it was for.

POTHECARY. I know. But I don't believe you. I think you're mocking us.

P.-P. It's true. I'm a lost child.

POTHECARY. But you're a V.I.P. A V.I.P. can't be a lost child.

P.-P. He's never anything else.

[POTHECARY *is going to say something but checks herself.*

[56]

POTHECARY.   I must go.   Don't see me out, I know the way.

P.-P.   Of course I'll see you out.

> > *[They go out as—*

> *[The Prologue* ACT DROP *falls and the lights dim to black.*

> *[The lights rise on an evening scene in front of* P.-P.'s *bungalow.   A street lamp is lit* R.   *Under it stands* JOEY MASCARA *with his overcoat buttoned up. Rather sinister music is softly played, as if from a gramophone in one of the bungalows.*

JOEY (*to the lamp-post*).   Lux in tenebris, there's nobody
    but you and me,
And the whispering, incomprehensible Sea.
The Bungalists of Baikie are having their tea.
No moon.   Clouds veil the girn and the grin of
    Astarte.
I'll expound to ye, Lamp, the Pounce-Pellott's party.

When Pontius Pilate cam hame frae the East,
What did he find ?   What did he find ?
Bewilderment, doubt and a fog of the mind
In the places lang syne he had left behind.
Allah, the Disheveller, had been there afore him.
The proud had been scattered in the imagination of
    their hearts,
And the Mighty been coupit from their seats.

The temples were gutted and the ornaments from the
    altars
Were heapit like junk in the streets.
Honour and glory, dominion and power, a' things
    high and holy,
Were a' gien owre to the poor and the lowly.
The tarnished swords, the battered sceptres,

The immemorial things,
Were waving in the hands and roond the heids o' the
    new kings.
The meek had inherited the earth.
What would they dae wi' it?

When Pontius Pilate came back frae the East
He called a Feast that wasna a Feast.

For the magistrate's doup maun aye be on the seat of
    judgement;
He may smile and play the host; but there's aye a
    cause in his hied.
Pilate, wi' hinging lip and sweet urbanity,
Has come a second time to judge humanity.

Dod, and he'll mak a bonny moagger o't, as he
Done afore . . . But whit was he to dae?

For the things that were done in the green tree
They are daeing again in the dry;
And what can he say but, " See ye to it "?
And wash.   And let them die.

> [*He goes out, whistling* The Flowers of the Forest.

> [*The moon is uncovered, and the* DEVIL'S MASK *appears,
> grinning.*

> [*The lights in the bungalow go brilliantly up and, to
> loud and prolonged music, the* GUESTS *arrive and are
> admitted by* BABY. JOEY *comes last and kisses*
> BABY *enthusiastically before the door is shut and the*
> ACT DROP *lifted. This last little incident is accom-
> panied by* THE DE'IL'S *voice, loudly intoning :*

THE DE'IL.   None but the Brave,
None but the Brave,
None but the Brave deserve the Fair.

The fare is paid,
The preparations made,
The Banquet laid.
Get tore into it, my hellhounds, my hearties.

[*Except for the electric fire and a light from the semi-open doorway, the parlour is dark when the* DROP *goes up.*

[*Laughter is heard and* LADY MAGGIE *enters, followed by* JUDY.

JUDY.   Wait a minute.   I'll put on the lights.

[JUDY *switches on the lights.*   JEMIMA *and* DR. POTHE-CARY *follow in ; then* BABY *with a coffee-tray.*

MAGGIE.   Isn't this a little like some play or other by poor little Sir James Barrie ?
JUDY.   Oh ?   Is it ?
JEMIMA.   Did you know Barrie, Lady Margaret ?
MAGGIE.   Oh, yes.   Everybody did.   We all went to a party at his flat in the Adelphi on my seventh birthday. He called me his favourite villainess.   I was only seven.
JEMIMA.   Why did he call you that ?
MAGGIE.   I expect it was some kind of joke.   He was very witty.

[*Coffee is served.*

POTHECARY.   That was a most marvellous dinner, Lady Pellott.
JUDY.   You must thank Mrs. Crowe for that.   Nobody ever told me American women were so wonderful.
JEMIMA.   We struggle around and make do. . . . But I thought it was a good idea, having it in your most charming little kitchen.
POTHECARY.   I think your greatest feat was making the men wash up.
JUDY.   Oh, that wasn't so difficult.   Since we came

home, Jim has been a lovely scullery-maid. I loved
Ketch's face, though, when Mrs. Crowe chucked him a
towel.

POTHECARY. I thought he was going to walk out.
He's a councillor, you see, Lady Margaret. A very proud
man.

MAGGIE. Those thingummibobs, wrapped in white of
egg—like summer clouds. I almost saw angels with
wings and golden crowns sitting about on them. I hope
I shall dream about them, and where did you get the
eggs ?

JEMIMA. Oh, we got around a bit this afternoon.

MAGGIE. I feel almost happy . . . " linking lythly
widdershins : Ring-a-ring-a-widdershins : Round go we."

JUDY. I beg your pardon ?

MAGGIE. It's a rhyme an old Nannie of mine taught me.
Bless my soul, what a squint she had ! I can see it, or
them, or whatever you call a squint, still. Do you think
squints are unlucky, dear ?

BABY. I don't know.

MAGGIE. Something must have been unlucky.

POTHECARY. You're thinking of the Evil Eye.

MAGGIE. Am I ? I don't think so.

JEMIMA. It's all superstition.

MAGGIE. I like superstition.

JUDY. What a bore Doctor Beadle is.

JEMIMA. I wonder. I think he *has* some fun in him.
But I didn't know your Scottish clergymen were so awful
strict. He might just as well be a Roman Catholic.

POTHECARY. Just as well. I don't see anything but a
technical difference between the whole boiling of them.

JEMIMA. Now, now. We mustn't be profane, must
we ?

MAGGIE. Cosmo Lang told me I was an awful heathen.
That was because I laughed at his gaiters. It was thought-
less of me ; but it was a long time ago. He was only
Archbishop of York then.

JEMIMA. Those poor men. I wonder how they are getting on.

JUDY. Go and help them, Baby.

BABY. Righty-oh.

[*Exit* BABY.

JEMIMA. What a pretty, nice girl she is ! You must send her to me. We have a lot of fine young men coming about our home in Spottsville.

JUDY. She'd be spoiled.

JEMIMA. And so what ? I spent my teen ages being spoiled and liked it. And look at me. I'm not exactly ruined.

MAGGIE (*looking at her*). No. I should say that, in a sense, that's quite true.

JEMIMA. On this side your girls are all clewed up with inhibitions. I've always been a good girl, and yet I've never had an inhibition in my life.

POTHECARY. Well, now, I wonder if that can be strictly accurate.

JEMIMA. I am not in the habit of being inaccurate, Doctor. That was one thing my father never could abide. Inaccuracy. Mother, too. So any kind of slovenly thinking or a casual way with figures and things is that which I have avoided all through my entire existence. I hope you'll believe that. . . . And here are our weary galley-slaves . . .

[*Enter severally* BEADLE, COPPER, KETCH *and* P.-P.
BABY *and* JOEY *are absent*.

JEMIMA. How's tricks, boys ?

BEADLE. We got through our allotted tasks very quickly. Sir James is a born leader.

JUDY. Have you had coffee ?

BEADLE. Yes, yes, yes, yes. Even that.

JUDY. Now, do make yourselves comfortable. . . .

[*With some fuss*, ALL *sit*.

Where's Baby ?

P.-P.   She and Mascara are putting the things away.
JUDY.   Oh!

[*She looks a little worried.*

[*P.-P. hands round cigarettes.   A pause.*

JEMIMA.   What were you all talking about, in there?
COPPER.   We had no time to talk.   It's a good thing
Sir James didn't come back to the Home Civil Service.
He'd have killed us all in no time.
MAGGIE.   Would he?   Would he?
COPPER.   I bet he would.
MAGGIE.   Ah!

[*She lapses into the contemplation of happy vistas.*

[*Another slight pause.*

JUDY.   Polly, I wish you'd tell Baby not to mind.   We
can put the things away in the morning.
P.-P.   All right.   If you like.

[*P.-P. goes out.*

JEMIMA.   Forgive me, but I have to laugh.   You've so
got your old feudal system in your bones, you get all
hotted up and locoed over a simple little supper party.
You hide it, but it's there.   Now look: I've got three
establishments (forgive me) a sight more pretentious than
this, and I conduct them with the assistance of a hired
coloured girl and her illegitimate daughter (pardon me,
Doctor Beadle).   The rest is done by the simple appreci-
ation of logistics enjoyed on our side of the Atlantic
Ocean.   Now, it's not for me to instruct you in any way,
God forbid, but surely . . . *surely* . . .

[*A crash of breaking crockery.   JUDY screams.*

JUDY.   Oh, my God!   Captain Copper, please go to
[62]

them. He's beating the man, and he's terribly strong, though he doesn't look it. He'll kill the little wretch!

[COPPER *goes, but is met by* BABY, *perfectly composed.*

Baby! What's the matter? What are they doing?

BABY It's all right, Mother, don't make an exhibition of yourself. Joey was a little startled. There isn't much broken. Polly's got the dustpan and brush. Do sit down, everybody.

JUDY. I'm so sorry. . . . For a moment I thought. . . . Do forgive me for being so silly. My abominable nerves!

BABY. It's only a couple of plates. They were cracked anyway.

COPPER. I'll see whether I can help.

[*Exit* COPPER.

POTHECARY. A couple of plates is serious enough, these days.

MAGGIE. If your dinner set *is* spoiled, I think I could let you have a rather nice set of Staffordshire that belonged to my mother. I saw it somewhere only yesterday. We could have it valued, or we could just come to an agreement. I know nothing about money.

JUDY. That's awfully kind of you, Lady Maggie; but I don't think it can be as bad as that.

BABY. No. It isn't. It's only two plates.

[*Re-enter* COPPER, JOEY *and* P.-P.   P.-P. *is under some restraint.*

POTHECARY. You gave us all a fright, Sir James.

P.-P. Did I? I'm sorry. There's practically no damage done.

JOEY. We had a little accident.

P.-P. No real damage done.

JEMIMA. That's a mercy.

[*General settling down.*

P.-P. Perhaps I ought to explain why I didn't thrash this fellow within an inch of his life and kick him along the promenade.

JUDY.⎱ Polly, for Heaven's sake . . .
BABY.⎰ That's not fair . . .

P.-P. It may be the new way of living to accept a man's hospitality and attempt to seduce his daughter. I don't know. But I want to find out. I want to find out a lot of things.

BEADLE. I must remind you that I warned you about Mr. Mascara's . . . proclivities.

P.-P. I know you did.

MAGGIE. But, dear me, there's nothing new about it !

JOEY. I'd better go.

P.-P. You'll go when I tell you to go. Sit down, you stupid little swine.

[JOEY *makes a deprecatory gesture and sits.*

BABY. Look here, Daddy . . .

P.-P. Be good enough to be seen and not heard. . . . Ladies and gentlemen, I'm sorry if this little incident has embarrassed you. It has embarrassed me. But it may serve as a starting point for our discussion.

KETCH. I object.

P.-P. To what do you object, Mr. Ketch ?

KETCH. I object to the continued presence of Mr. Mascara.

P.-P. He is my guest.

KETCH. I don't care whether he's your guest or not. It's not for me to say, but a wee while ago, at some personal inconvenience, I pulled a wee lassie out of the ditch. You told all these people that, and I didna like it; but never mind that. I didna do what I did for his sordid satisfactions and if you're feared to hammer Hell out of him, I'm not . . . (*to* JOEY) . . . Come outside.

P.-P. Sit down, Ketch. I've got the floor.

[64]

KETCH.   Oh, whatever you say.   But he can take that grin off his face.

P.-P.   Once upon a time,
 Or many times upon many times,
 The East fell to pieces.
 The jungle vines tore her water tanks;
 The desert sand covered her canals;
 The wild pig rooted in her palaces.

 The Wisdom of the East is that it is all no good.
 Mankind are thieves and liars and murderers and
  oppressors,
 And disease and famine we have always with us
 And we must shift as we can till Death comes to
  take us.
 Who knows what the gods have in mind ?

 The sun sets later in the West
 And we have not come upon such wisdom.
 It is ours to seek and to find,
 To invent, to manipulate
 Rocks, rivers, metals, bodies and souls;
 To channel and to build,
 To master the earth and the waters and the sky,
 To organise our mastery.

 In our search we found the East
 And brought with us the will to exist,
 The illusion of continuing existence,
 And seized and held on and arranged
 With our firm, clever hands;
 Forcing back pestilence and famine;
 Teaching our thoughts which were not thoughts at
  all but an urging passion.

 To a vast, ancient land,
 Made ours by cunning and courage and force of arms,

They sent me, Pontius Pilate, to teach and to rule.
They chose me from many.
I was packed full of learning.
I knew self-denial.
They sent me to teach and to rule.
To school the men of the East to seek and to find,
To invent and manipulate,
And to rule themselves, when the Great Day came,
The Day when the passion of the West found its
    apotheosis,
When the dragon was cast down and death and
    Hell
Cast into the lake of fire.

" Now," said we, " by precept and example
" We have shown you how men rule themselves.
" Take back your land and our God be with you
" As ever He is with us."

So Pilate is home again, his occupation gone.
Bewildered by change and frightened by the lingering
    sharp smell of ashes.
Be kind to him and take him by the hand.
Guide him through the Millennium.

[*There is a short silence till* COPPER *shifts uneasily in his
    seat, then coughs and gives tongue.*

COPPER.   Well, Sir James, you've put a few points to us
that are maybe a bit unusual; and I'm not saying but
that some of the heid yins in the Service with their pin-
stripe breeks and attaché cases would be stuck to find an
answer.   But some of us Civil Servants nowadays are
men of the world too, and no' too much tied up with
precedents.   Maybe you'll not mind if I'm a wee bit
informal.   On the other hand, you're not to take anything
I say between these four walls as in any way binding on
my Department. . . . Chrrrm.

[66]

Well now, administration's not so easy as it was in your young days, and we've different problems to solve than what you had in India, when you just had to clap your hands and a babu came running. We have to apply Social Science.

It's true we've got Regulations to help us; but the Regulations themselves have grown so beautifully intricate that it would take a College of Cardinals to interpret them. We have to employ certain broad, general principles. The sheep dog doesna ken muckle about rearing and selling sheep; but he applies broad, general principles.

What are these principles?

P.-P. You told me. Keep them on the move.

COPPER. Now, now. You mustn't take me up on unguarded expressions let drop in a lighter moment. Civilisation is a large and delicate instrument. For example, take the flow of commodities. A thousand channels have to be designed, prepared, noted, checked, kept in repair—in a word, " planned." And skilfully controlled.

[JOEY *belches.*

JOEY. Pardon me.

COPPER. Granted. . . . Now, clearly this planning and control is a matter for experts. I don't mean experts in channels or commodities. There's plenty of them. Their job in the modern state is to take orders. I mean experts in planning and controlling.

JOEY. Who are these experts?

COPPER. I'm coming to that. They're not politicians.

JOEY. Hear, hear.

COPPER. The politician's function (when he's a Minister) is to protect the men who are doing the job from interference; to keep the public happy with speeches; to take advice; to give decisions; and to Govern.

JOEY. Who told them they could govern?

COPPER. Eh?

JOEY. I'm saying, who gave them permission to
govern anything? They're supposed to be a Ministry.
That means a collection of servants.   Doctor Beadle here'll
tell you that a servant when he ruleth is an abomination in
the sight of the Lord.

COPPER.   We are not discussing religion.

BEADLE.   Not yet.

COPPER.   What you want is anarchy.

JOEY.   Never mind what I want.   There are only two
sanctions for ruling people.   One is that they're dangerous
criminals and the other is that you've knocked their
country flat with cannons and bombs.   You and your
politicians have neither of these sanctions for ruling us.
This is a democracy.   If that means anything it means
that you're to do what we tell you; not that we're to do
what you tell us.

BEADLE.   There must be a degree of discipline.

JOEY.   That's what the Law is for.

JEMIMA.   But politicians make the Laws.

JOEY.   They try to.   Just you go into any Court and
listen to the Judge and the Jury trying to warstle their
handiwork into common sense.   But all right.   Let them
get on with it.   Only don't let them take the Law into
their own hands.   Their own piggy hands.

BEADLE.   I was not aware that you respected any Law of
God or man.

JOEY.   Every artist kens fine there are Laws.   Every
artist has to accept them.   What I'm beefing about is a
dozen stupid rules a day and a wee bully with a heap of
forms up every street to enforce them.

COPPER.   Man, you don't understand the first thing
about Social Science.

JOEY.   Except that it is not a science at all.

COPPER.   What next?   You'll be saying psychology's
not a science.

JOEY.   No more it is.

POTHECARY.   Ignorance.   Just plain ignorance.   I

[68]

think we've heard just about enough from you, Mister Joseph Mascara.

JOEY.   You've not heard anything yet.

P.-P. (*violently*).   None of us has heard anything yet. Stop this damned nonsense.   Don't you realise I'm in earnest ?

COPPER.   Sir James, I sympathise fully with your feelings.   They say it's impossible to draw a straight line freehand.   It's almost impossible to get things straight when a lot of ignoramuses are joggling your elbow. We're trying to get things straight.   These statutory orders and regulations are only our instruments.   Give us a chance.   If a surgeon's straightening your leg, you don't start criticising his hammers and chisels.   We *know* they're damned sore.   We give you all the anæsthetic we can, short of killing you with dope.   You don't see the open wound.   You only feel it.   You'll never get anywhere unless you trust the chaps that can see it.

POTHECARY.   Yes.   But I'd rather know that the surgeon has got his F.R.C.S.

JOEY.   A bloody row of bloody letters.

BEADLE.   There are ladies present.

JOEY.   Oh, God bless them ! . . . All right, all right. I'm an A.R.C.M., if it comes to that.   And if you want any more, I'm an R.S.W.   But God forgive me if I start laying down the law on the strength of that.

JEMIMA.   On the strength of what do you start laying down the law, Mr. Mascara ?

JOEY.   There you have me.

MAGGIE.   My aunt used to lay down the law because her father was a Marquis.   So was mine, as a matter of fact. I never lay down the law, but I wonder, sometimes, whether there is anything in it.

KETCH.   In what ?

MAGGIE.   Oh, I don't know.   It's quite biological, in a way, isn't it, Doctor Pothecary ?

POTHECARY.   Well, maybe it is and maybe it isn't.   It

depends on how much dominant is passed down in the gene.

KETCH. Mr. Chairman, I submit this is irrelevant. Nobody listens to Marquises nowadays.

MAGGIE. Oh yes, they do.

JUDY. But being a Marquis gave a sort of mystic authority didn't it ? Doesn't Mr. Mascara want to know where the authority comes from nowadays.

COPPER. From the ballot-box.

JUDY. But haven't you said yourself that the people aren't capable of looking after themselves ?

COPPER. Well, suppose they aren't. They choose people who *can* look after them.

JUDY. How ?

COPPER. You mean how do they choose them ?

JUDY. Yes.

JOEY. I'll tell you. A dozen busybodies meet in a schoolroom and make a choice between two or three blethers who're idle enough to want to get into Parliament. Then another bunch of busybodies pick who is to stand up and tell him he's a liar. Then the chap who talks best is sent to London with a thousand a year. One of six hundred or so. Two cliques pick themselves out of the six hundred and each of them says who is to be boss of two hundred or three hundred blethers. Once they've picked the bosses, they've got to do what they say, or they'll no' get a job. And as all these chaps know damn all about anything, they have to take the say-so of Mr. Copper, here, who isn't elected at all—maybe hasna even to pass an examination. There's your modern democracy for you.

COPPER. But it works.

JOEY. Like hell, it works.

JEMIMA. Certainly it works. It ensures that those who are willing to take Government seriously can get on with it. You, Mr. Mascara, have every opportunity of using your undoubted powers of expression in praise or

criticism of your elected representatives. In the mean-
time, government of the people for the people and by the
people has not yet perished from the earth. And thank
God for it. If it shows signs of doing so, the people can
give their governors the bums' rush. In my country
that's what they do.

JOEY. We can't here.

COPPER. Listen. You're always yelling for security.
Well, that's the only way to get security. Short of a
dictatorship.

JOEY. We've got a dictatorship.

POTHECARY. Now, now.

JOEY. No now, now, about it. And where's the
security? Copper's here to protect us from War, Famine
and Pestilence. Government has no other proper function. None. Sir James did that in India, as well as he
could. Well, you've not protected us from war. And
famine and pestilence are bearing down on us like charging
elephants. Famine and pestilence can't read. Your buff
forms are no good against them.

JEMIMA. You appear to hold a strong hand in destruc-
tive criticism, Mr. Mascara; but I don't find that you are
very, very constructive. What is your solution?

JOEY. Let us alone. That's all. Let us alone while
we can still blow our own noses.

COPPER. I suppose letting you alone would fill your
bellies with wheat and meat from the four quarters of the
globe?

JOEY. We got them before there was a blinking Ministry
of blooming food.

JEMIMA. There's more of you now and less food.

KETCH. And only some of you got what there was.

COPPER. You want to do just what you blooming well
like, do you?

JOEY. Yes. Of course I do. And so does everybody.
And how do you weaver-kneed little blokes in offices know
that what we want isn't the right thing?

[71]

COPPER. We're there to give you what you want—within reason.

JOEY. Within whose reason?

P.-P. There is nothing in this I couldn't get in a third-class carriage. Have you nothing to tell me?

BEADLE. Yes.

P.-P. Well, then, tell me.

BEADLE. I will.

P.-P. Then go ahead.

BEADLE. What we have heard is the confused cry of " Lo, here; lo there!" Of which we have information from the Holy Scriptures.

MAGGIE. What did you say?

BEADLE. I referred to the Holy Scriptures.

MAGGIE. No, before that.

BEADLE. Lo, here; lo, there?

MAGGIE. Yes. Thank you. Please go on.

BEADLE. The Church has the answer to it all. That is all I have to say.

JEMIMA. You mean that's all?

BEADLE. Yes.

JEMIMA. Oh!

KETCH. Just plain, blunt dogma, eh?

BEADLE. It is not for a Communist to talk to me about dogma.

KETCH. And what do you mean by that, eh? Ride off on a damned insult, is that your idea, eh? Dialectical materialism is dogma, is it? Look here, Doctor Beadle, you may be a very holy and sacred figure to your congregation of superstitious dopes, but I'm not one of them. You can button your collar behind your neck till you're black in the face, but it makes no impression on me, see. You'll take that back.

BEADLE. Bless my soul, what *am* I to take back? You don't subscribe to a dogma, then?

KETCH. Of course I don't.

BEADLE. I'm sorry, I thought you did.

KETCH.   I'm convinced, if that's what you mean.

BEADLE.   I know.   You believe.   You have faith.

KETCH.   I nothing of the sort have.   I'm intellectually
convinced.   I've got conviction.   Through reason.

BEADLE.   I see.   We call that belief, you know.

KETCH.   You can call it a sky-blue panda if you like.
It's not the same thing.

BEADLE.   You're right.   It isn't.   What you call conviction is hypnotic automatism.   Does that definition suit
you better ?

KETCH.   But that's what your belief is.

MAGGIE.   What is hypnotic automatism ?

POTHECARY.   The behaviour of people under hypnosis.
Do you know, I think they're both quite right.

KETCH.   You don't like Communism, eh ?

BEADLE.   I certainly do not.

KETCH.   You don't like logical solutions.

BEADLE.   It depends what they are.

KETCH.   Pick and choose, eh ?

BEADLE.   We have a certain freedom of choice.

KETCH.   Not here, you haven't.   It's coming.   You'll
have to like it or lump it.

[BEADLE *takes on an almost pontifical magnificence.*

BEADLE.   Haha !   You threaten Christendom ?
    But you will find us like a strong man, armed.
    Christendom is prepared.

KETCH.   The other cheek is ready ?

BEADLE.   We have gone far to dislocate our necks
    Turning the other cheek.   Peace, if you will.
    But if you choose to play the Jingiz Khan
    And loose your shabby savages on the West,
    We'll drive the slant-eyed atheists down to Hell
    And blow your blood-built Kremlin into shards.

KETCH.   The way the Germans did in '44.

BEADLE.   They were not Christian soldiers.

F   [73]

KETCH.   Be your age.
  Go home and read the Sermon on the Mount.
JEMIMA.   These sacred words are very, very grand;
  But hardly applicable to the present times.
BEADLE.   I can't agree with that.
JEMIMA.   Excuse me, please.
  I'm certain, if Our Lord had thought of it,
  He would have been the earliest to admit
  That if a pack of hoodlums should get tough
  The only answer is to play it rough.
BEADLE.   Let us not be misled because her words
  Carry a prairie air that seems profane.
  Within my mind I see the knotted rope
  Swung by a strong young carpenter.   I see . . .
  I see the fluttering feathers; hear the crash
  Of falling cash desks in the Temple porch.
KETCH.   And so you have it both ways.   Carry on.
  Live in your Never Never Never Land
  Of bourgeois fairy stories.   Stop your ears,
  And maybe you'll shut out the tramping feet
  Of the class-conscious proletariat.
  Hushabye, babies, high on the tree top,
  Dream on your dreams and tak nae heed o' the roots
  Crumbling to rotten powder down ablow ye.
  " Balow, my bairns, your Daddy's gone a hunting
  To get a rabbit skin for Baby Bunting,
  Daddy wad mak ye spruce and warm and furry;
  Daddy wad mak ye bien and proud and rich;
  Balow, my babe, dinna be in a hurry,
  For Daddy's lying cauld and died in a ditch."
MAGGIE.   How very horrible !   Really, Mr. Ketch !
JEMIMA.   Daddy is sitting on the banks of the Potomac,
  Perfectly cosy with a great big gun.
KETCH.   Aye, the murdering warmonger !   But no sae
cosy.
  P.-P.   So the Russian Empire is not for War ?
  KETCH.   What do you mean by the Russian Empire ?

P.-P.   What we've always meant by the Russian Empire. Answer my question, please.

KETCH.   If you mean the Union of Democratic Socialist Republics, the answer's easy.   They've had some. They've just won a war at the expense of ten million young men.   What would they want wi' a war ?

JUDY.   I'm glad of that.   A war isn't a very satisfactory solution of anything, is it ?   Do you want a war, Doctor Beadle ?

BEADLE.   No, of course not.

JUDY.   You, Mrs. Crowe ?

JEMIMA.   I most certainly do not.

JOEY.   There are worse things than war.

POTHECARY.   We haven't seen a real war yet, have we ? Not with the hydrogen bomb and bacteriology.

JUDY.   Don't let's talk about it.   Nobody but Mr. Mascara wants it, so why should we have it ?

JOEY.   Because we're wedged between two solid blocks of blasted fanatics.

JUDY.   You mustn't call Doctor Beadle and Mr. Ketch fanatics.

JOEY.   What are they, then ?

Old Beadle found a baby in a byre
Who grew to be a poet and talked sense.
Beadle forgot the sense
And he twisted the poetry till no sane man could believe a word of it.
He crusted the wean's crib with diamonds
And slammed the door on the four Wise Men.
And deaved his Creator wi' sickening flattery continually.

Young Ketch found a hope for the poor and wretched
In a system for binding the bullies in chains.
And now, by Heavens, we're all in chains,
With a new lot of bullies ettling to stamp
The human spirit deeper in the mud.

[75]

The Medes and the Persians had nothing on these
twa.

To Hell with them both.

KETCH.   So that's what you think?

JOEY.   That's what I think.

BEADLE.   You dinna believe in Divine Revelation?

JOEY.   I do when I see it.   The world itsel's miracle
enough for me.   You can keep your conjuring tricks.

BEADLE.   You do not believe in miracles?

Have you considered the miracle of all miracles?
The miracle that changed the people of Europe
From bloodthirsty brutes to men and women?

JOEY.   They are still bloodthirsty brutes.

BEADLE (*disregarding him*).   Lovers of each other,
Lovers of sanity,
Lovers of law,
Lovers of beauty.
Florence was built in Nazareth.
Justice was born in Bethlehem.
The beast-gods died,
And the Man-God rose from the dead.

JUDY.   And now you shut the golden doors on
us;
And now they shut the iron doors on us;
And behind the doors they whisper and scheme.

P.-P.   If you persist in being wise and good,
I shall have nothing to complain about.
Go on, you talkative fools.
I am a bewildered man.   Tell me what I have to
do?

KETCH.   What is this talk of gods?
All that we know are men.
We teach that Man must fulfil himself.
What is there else to do?

BEADLE.   The sun is material; the horizon is material.
When the sun blots out the horizon,
Where then will be your materialists?

[76]

KETCH. Done and dead. But there are years to go
before that time.
And who knows but we shall master
The sun and the horizon.

JOEY. What do you mean by " we " ?
More thaumaturgists, more priests,
Why can't you leave it to the artist and the poet ?
For God speaks to him through his great red lugs,
God makes signals to him through his parboiled
eyes.

BEADLE. The artist has no authority.

KETCH. The artist has no authority. What have you
told us tonight ?

BEADLE. God spoke to Saint Paul in a blazing light.
Has he spoken that way to you ?

JOEY. God spoke to Elijah in a still, small voice,
Urgent, incomprehensible.
Listen to the voice, you bloody fool,
Listen to the voice.
In time you may understand it.

JEMIMA. You have spoken to us pretty frequently
In a loud and aggressive voice.
I should be the last to decry immortal Art;
But I find it infernally unintelligible.
" An infant crying in the night "
(As it has been delightfully expressed by one of your
poets)
" And with no language save a cry."
I respectfully submit that you
Had better provide us with a code;
Or else forgive us for thinking
That it is the wind or an open safety-pin.

POTHECARY. Why don't you leave it to us ?

JOEY. Eh ?

COPPER. Yes. Or us. We don't pretend to be able to
look at the back of the book for the answers.

JUDY. Perhaps there are no answers.

COPPER. Perhaps not.

P.-P. Why is a raven like a writing-desk? And the answer is, " I haven't the slightest idea."

MAGGIE. But that answer is intolerable. I can't believe that anything was meant to be intolerable. Mr. Huxley once told me that there was such a thing as summation of stimuli. A thing can go on beating at our nervous system until our nervous system refuses to answer. We can bear anything till we become unconscious. And then we wake up and start all over again. So Mr. Huxley said. But to say that there is no solution at the end of the book is what Mr. Bernard Shaw once called in my hearing, a knock-out. We have no experience of it, therefore why should we have to admit that it may be true? . . . Dear me, I seem to be talking a great deal.

POTHECARY. Then why don't you let us go on asking questions and testing the answers?

COPPER. Why must you jump off the bus when it's taking you somewhere?

BEADLE. Life isn't a bus; and the answer has already been given.

JOEY. Not by a long chalk, it hasn't.

BABY. No. Joey's quite right. It hasn't.

JUDY. Baby, darling!

BABY. I didn't want to come into this bloody world.

JUDY. Baby!

BABY. The best thing Polly ever did was to pitch me over the rail into the sea. But Mr. Ketch, it seems, pulled me out. Very well, then. Here I am. Thousands of people tell me things. They tell me how to do this and how to do that and everything except how to avoid being damned miserable, and it's easy enough to know why they don't tell me that. They're all damned miserable themselves. At least, the people are who tell me how to do things. You're all old. You've forgotten what it is to be young. It's like recovering from frostbite. It's damned sore.   All your faculties are waking up, body, soul and spirit.   And they give you Hell.

Very well, then.   I don't know what in the blazes I'm here for, but the least I can do is to make it bearable. I can listen to Bela Bartok and Shostakovich, because they tell me that a time will come when all I'm suffering will be rather fun.   That a kick on the stomach can be as jolly as a cornet of ice-cream.   I *like* being kissed and cuddled by that little bounder Joey, though he smells like an unwashed spaniel, and I know what he says about me being exciting and clever and beautiful is so much sales talk.   It takes me from one empty hour to the other.   It keeps me from worrying what it's all about with nothing in my blooming nut to make all my worrying useful and profitable.

I know, I know.   I'll get married and be a cow and look at the trains over a barbed-wire fence for ever and ever, amen.

JUDY.   Baby, I think you've had too much drambuie.

BABY.   Perhaps I have.   I've had too much of everything.   I'm spiritually sick and perhaps you'd better wipe it up and say no more about it.

[*She rushes from the room.*

JUDY (*suddenly blazing*).   There you are.   That's what you clever people have given to the younger generation. It's your fault as much as anyone's, Doctor Beadle.

BEADLE.   I fail to see how it can possibly be my fault. If you had brought the child up properly . . .

JUDY.   I know how to bring children up properly.   I was brought up properly myself.   My father and my mother taught me the difference between right and wrong and jolly well took care that I did right.   And you were at the back of it, Doctor Beadle, with your nice, long, soothing, incomprehensible sermons.   My father and mother came to you every Sunday to hear you say, " Carry on, Serjeant-Major."   There was no *doubt*.   God gave the middle classes each day their daily bread and a baker to cook it and a nice polite maid to put it on the table.   My God, in those days there was *somebody* who could run steadily on the tram-lines.   And that's better than nowadays when there's nobody.   We're told what to do by people who couldn't even keep their children from getting rickets.

POTHECARY.   But you must remember that your sort of home life was a perfect hotbed of complexes.

JUDY.   I don't care.   I may be bursting with complexes; but I'd rather be that than feel as Baby feels now.

POTHECARY.   But that's what's the matter with *her*.

JUDY.   Look here, Doctor Pothecary, I don't want to be rude, but I've listened to as much nonsense tonight as I can bear.

POTHECARY.   Oh, of course, in that case . . .

JEMIMA.   *My* method with *my* little girl . . .

JUDY.   And I don't want to hear about that either.

JEMIMA.   Well, I must say . . .

P.-P.   I think you must be tolerant with all three of us. You see, we're not very happy.

JEMIMA.   Why, for the land's sake, not ?   According to your lights, you've done a good deal of good, though it may have been for a mistaken imperialistic policy, and you're back home, wreathed in laurels.   You may have been shabbily treated on the financial side, but, with all modesty, I may say I've stepped in and put all that right.   I don't ask for thanks.   I merely indicate the facts.   Then why worry?   But I expect you don't like me, Sir James.   You're one of those men that don't like taking favours from girls.

POTHECARY.   You're right about him, in a way.   He's got very strong aggressive instincts—almost psychopathic.   He's had to keep them in control; but mind you, although he worked out his aggression on the Hindus and the tigers and things, it's very significant that he dropped his daughter overboard.   You mustn't be surprised at his attitude, Mrs. Crowe.   When I started on him he had a very strong negative transference indeed, though he's by no means under-sexed, and I think, in

time, the attraction will more than balance the repulsion.
What we've got to do with him is . . .

JUDY.   The man happens to be my husband.   I will not
have you two tabby cats fighting over him as if he were
a fish head.

POTHECARY.   But you don't understand, Lady Pellott.

JUDY.   I know that.   And I don't want to.

JEMIMA.   This is the first occasion on which I have ever
been alluded to as a tabby cat.   It seems to me to betray a
most extraordinary attitude.

P.-P.   I do not want you, Mrs. Crowe.
     I don't know why it should be so;
     But
     I do not want you, Mrs. Crowe.
     I have the impulse to be free.
     You cosset me and pamper me,
     Maternally and tactfully.
     I like you very much.   But, no.
     I do not want you, Mrs. Crowe.

     I do not want you, Doctor Jean,
     Although I gather what you mean;
     But
     I do not want you, Doctor Jean.
     For all that I have known and done
     You split to one, and one and one . . .
     I think it is by no means plain
     That you can put me together again;
     And, anyhow, I'll eat my hat
     If I'm so simple as all that.
     So, while I tread this mortal scene,
     I do not want you, Doctor Jean.

     It would be neither true nor proper
     To say I want you, Mr. Copper.
     Another one I do not want
     Is Lady Maggie Revenant.

[81]

And as for you, delightful Joe,
My answer must again be, no.
Though I should be the last to grudge
Your claim to be your only judge,
Your notions are confused and muddy;
Your unbowed head is pretty bloody;
I find the skipper of your soul
A little short of self-control
And far too ready to commute
And be a playful prostitute.
Your hedonism and anarchy,
Alas, make no appeal to me.
Your harp has made the Halls of Tara
An intellectual Saharah.
I do not want you, Joe Mascara.

[*The lights dim. As each character is dismissed by*
P.-P., *he or she retires to the background.*

[P.-P. *puts an arm round* JUDY *and* BABY. BABY *having
re-entered.*

[*On either side of the family group* BEADLE *and* KETCH
are sitting grimly on chairs slewed round to face it.

[*Raises his voice.*

The upper and nether millstones are closing upon me.
I am a living man and they are more or less natural objects.
Slowly and steadily they rotate and advance.
Must I stand and be squashed like a bug?

I know order and I know disorder.
Order I have forever loved and ensued.
Here and there I have imposed order upon this eel-pit
of a world.
My order could move within itself, orderly,
Propagate and increase in peace.
This is the order of two dead stones—
Two dead, flat stones, pieces of machinery.

I will not lie down and be crushed by those horrible
    stones.
I will be a King and a Priest again.
I was a stupid priest and a dull king;
But an honourable king and an honest priest.
My realm was green and golden,
My parish was kindly and quiet.
My realm and my parish were not great granite
    abominations.
I never imagined Destruction, much less
Made Destruction my goal and my god.

I must stand up against the millstones.
I must split them in four with my human hands.
I must breathe once more.
Only once.

I have killed my wife and my child.
I have sold their bodies for honour;
    So I must be punished.

I have washed my hands of my God and killed
    Him.
I have sold Him for order.
    Therefore I must be punished.

But, by the God I sold, I will not go quietly.
Where is my Stick !

[*The lights flicker in rainbow colours. Drums. Loud,
squeaking, Punch and Judy music plays* Rule Britannia
in the minor. JUDY *and* BABY *run to and fro,
squealing softly.* P.-P. *cuts loose.*

Take that, Hangman : Take that, Beadle :
And you, Doctor, and you, Clown, and you, Jim
    Crow, take that, and that and that !

[*He kills the ladies and gentlemen mentioned with his stick. He is confronted by* LADY MAGGIE. *Silence.*

O Ghost !   What am I to do to you ?

MAGGIE.   I am terribly sorry; but you can do nothing to me.   I am a ghost, you see.

[*The lights have risen a little and there is a distant rumble. Enter* TOBY. *He stands respectfully with his hat in his hand, waiting for* P.-P. *to speak.* BABY *steals up behind him.*

P.-P.   Who are you ?

TOBY.   Toby Messan, apprentice plumber and electrician.

P.-P.   You are too young to die.

TOBY.   Nobody's too young for that, Mister.

P.-P.   I don't know who you are.

TOBY.   Neither does anybody, Mister.   Neither do I. You see, I've no richt begun, yet.

P.-P.   What do you want ?

TOBY.   I was thinking, if you've no objection, I'd like to marry your daughter.

BABY.   I would like that too.

P.-P.   It wasn't you who saved her life.   It was Ketch who saved her life.

TOBY.   No.   It wasn't me saved her.   But I've a notion I would like to.

P.-P. (*turning away*).   Very well.

[*As he goes upstage, soft music begins, only to be broken by a clash of cymbals as the* THE DE'IL *suddenly appears.*

Are you the Devil ?

THE DE'IL.   Aye. . . .   Weel, James MacArthur Pontius-Pilate, ye've had a braw bourackie hereaways.

P.-P.   Yes. . . .   Have you come to take me ?

THE DE'IL.   I was wondering.

P.-P.   I'm ready.

THE DE'IL. I'm thinking you've jouked me for the moment. It may be you've jinked me a' thegither. Time will tell us.

P.-P. Can I wait for time?

THE DE'IL. I dinna ken.

[*He vanishes.*

P.-P. If you don't know, who knows? Nobody
  knows. Nobody knows.
I've killed all those fools who pretended to know.
And so . . . and so . . .
With the soothsayers littered about the stage
That I slew in my rage,
Who did not know . . . and no more do I . . .
I must jest again and await my reply . . .

Good-bye.

CURTAIN

Printed in Great Britain by
RICHARD CLAY AND COMPANY, LTD.
BUNGAY
SUFFOLK

Brandane, John

THE GLEN IS MINE   Wrappers 3/- net
> A Highland comedy in three acts. 8m. 4f. Two
> interior scenes. Period : 1920

HEATHER GENTRY   Wrappers 3/6 net
> A comedy in three acts. 8m. 4f. Two interior
> scenes

THE INN OF ADVENTURE   Wrappers 3/6 net
> A comedy in three acts. 8m. 6f. One interior scene.
> Period : 1829

RORY AFORESAID and THE HAPPY WAR   Wrappers 2/6 net
> Containing :

RORY AFORESAID
> A comedy in one act. 5m. 1f. One interior scene
THE HAPPY WAR
> A play in one act. 5m. One interior scene. Period : 1917

Carroll, Sydney W.

THE IMPERIAL VOTARESS   Cloth 6/- net
> A chronicle play in twelve scenes with nine changes of
> scene. 41m. 14f. Period : 1548–1603 (Elizabethan)

Hamilton, Patrick

THE DUKE IN DARKNESS   Wrappers 5/- net
> A play in three acts. 10m. One interior scene.
> Period : 1580

GAS LIGHT   Wrappers 5/- net
> A Victorian thriller in three acts. 2m. 3f. One
> interior scene. Period : late Victorian

ROPE   Wrappers 5/- net
> A play in three acts. 6m. 2f. One interior scene

MONEY WITH MENACES. 11m. 8f.
TO THE PUBLIC DANGER. 6m. 3f.
> Two radio plays.   Wrappers 3/- net

Knox, Alexander

OLD MASTER   Cloth 6/-

A comedy in three acts.   16m. 10f.   Three interior scenes

Quinn, Hugh

MRS. MCCONAGHY'S MONEY AND OTHER PLAYS

Wrappers 3/- net

Containing :

MRS. MCCONAGHY'S MONEY

A play in three acts.   4m. 5f.   One interior scene.
Period : about 1917

A QUIET TWELFTH

A comedy in one act.   5m. 2f.   One interior scene.
Period : about 1915

COLLECTING THE RENT

A comedy in one act.   3m. 2f.   One exterior scene.
Period : about 1917

Sangster, Alfred

THE BRONTËS   Wrappers 3/6 net

A play in three acts.   10m. 7f.   Three interior scenes.   Period : 1840–1860

Shaw, Bernard

A list of Plays by Bernard Shaw, with number of players and period, will be sent on demand.

Williamson, Hugh Ross

MR. GLADSTONE   Wrappers 3/- net

A play in three acts.   9m. 2f.   Three interior scenes. Period : 1876–1894

QUEEN ELIZABETH   Wrappers 4/- net

A play in three acts.   7m. 3f.   One interior, one exterior scene.   Period : 1579–1584